A Woman's Experience, Strength and Hope

DON'T
GIVE UP
BEFORE
the Miracle

JON SUSAN RHODES

Quantum
Discovery
A LITERARY AGENCY

Don't Give Up Before the Miracle
Copyright © 2022 by Jon Susan Rhodes

ISBN
978-1-959314-84-4 (Paperback)
978-1-959314-85-1 (eBook)

This book is dedicated to:

The Fellowship of Alcoholics Anonymous

Table of Contents

Acknowledgements

I would like to acknowledge the enormous help and ceaseless hours given to me in creating this book. I wish to thank my cousin, Patti McCall, for her endless patience and guidance over the eight years it took to create this book

My dear friend, Claire Sinclair, never gave up on me, consistently advising me on the proper use of the English language in the first stages of my efforts.

Claire introduced me to Jayn Stewart, an editor in New Mexico, in 1998. For two solid years Jayn and I practically wore ourselves out coming and going to the post office, as she helped me organize the chapters and the book itself I owe both Claire and Jayn a big thanks.

Susan McCabe, a screenwriter with visual gifts, helped to add flavor and color to what I feared was a dull book, and I thank her for her enthusiastic input.

A special thanks to Victoria Giraud, my editor, who spent several months guiding me to give this project the final right touch.

Mostly, I owe a great deal of gratitude to my husband, Michael, for patiently and lovingly standing by me throughout this undertaking and believing in me all along.

Joni— Madrid, Spain 1952

Preface

At four o'clock in the morning, my alarm went off in my Ft. Lauderdale apartment. I shakily turned it off and got up to turn off my phone. No one had called so things were on schedule. I had parried the night before. Vaguely remembering that I had had a good time, I felt fortunate to have made it back into my own bed without passing out elsewhere.

I was due to report to crew scheduling at six-thirty sharp for an eight o'clock departure. I hoped the stinging beads of hot water in the shower would clear my head. First things first, so after I had dried off, I headed into the kitchen to mix a pitcher of margaritas. I used artificial sweetner for less calories and fresh-squeezed lime juice for lots of vitamin C.

While I packed my airline-issued suitcase, I sipped my drink. I was scheduled for a four-day trip that would lay over in Toronto, Puerto Rico and Atlanta, Georgia. It was February and I had to plan the right wardrobe for offduty time in the various climates-a heavy coat, scarf and boors for Toronto, a bathing suit and tropical attire for the Caribbean. I would need something in-between for Atlanta. When I was dressed, I looked in the mirror. I was pleased with my reflection. Even though I was petite, the stiff military-type uniform didn't diminish the trim lines of my figure. I looked flawless from the top of my brunette hairdo down to my polished high heels.

Despite my mood swings and a turbulent emotional life, I was happy working for Eastern Airlines, where I'd been for over ten years. I was an attractive and very feminine woman with an easy smile and a friendly manner, who needed a structured life. With its strict rules and regulations, Eastern Airlines offered me this kind of life. I felt safe and secure working for them. When I wanted a change of pace to travel or just to relax, I would apply for a month's leave of absence. I never questioned the fact that I had taken as many leaves as I could during the fifteen years I was employed by them. In all that time I had never worked a full year.

By five-thirty a.m., I was in my car and headed south for the crew parking lot at Miami International Airport. Punctuality was a must and always a challenge. I was written up as tardy and reported to my supervisor if only five minutes late. Fifteen minutes late meant replacement, and it only took three missed flights before termination. I had missed one flight in my first year of flight, which scared me so badly I became somewhat neurotic about getting to the airport on time. However, I was constantly badgered by my supervisor and crew scheduling for the rimes I was two or three minutes late. Those narrow misses made me drive dangerously on the interstate highways, but it never occurred to me to just leave my home earlier.

After I checked my company mailbox, which contained both company mail as well as personal mail, it was time for the crew briefing, which sometimes lasted for as long as thirty minutes. I usually chose to Ay the larger aircraft, where I could, more or less, get lost in the crowd of ten or more flight attendants. During these meetings we discussed which positions in the plane we were individually responsible for during boarding, in-flight and deplaning. Once char was over with, we boarded the aircraft.

I usually worked way in the back of the plane. My jump sear was close to the aft closet, which was where we could score passengers' items char had not been checked-in at the ticket counter and would not fit under the sears or in the overhead storage bins. It was where I stored my suitcase and my large company-issued purse. I kept a flask in my purse and made sure it was close at hand.

Before boarding, I would fix myself a stiff Bloody Mary with lots of lime. I'd chug it and chew the lime so there wouldn't be any telltale odor on my breath. The amount of drinks I cook depended on the length of the flight. I never wanted to appear tipsy or shaky. As far as I was concerned, I didn't have a problem with alcohol, it just helped me to relax so chat I appeared in control, and besides, I liked the effect alcohol had on me. If I was in one of my more "excitable" moods, it took a bit more alcohol. I didn't have a clue char I was treading the path of madness and alcohol addiction, and neither did my employers or fellow employees.

Things began to change one day when I bought a super-sized imperial quart of vodka in the duty-free shop at Toronto airport. I attached it to my "wheelie" containing my suitcase, and I thought it had gone unnoticed. The next morning, before boarding the plane, I bought another imperial quart. After this trip, when I was home on my day off, I received a call from my supervisor. She informed me I had been reported for alcohol abuse by the head flight attendant on my last flight. She told me to report immediately to the airline medical facility for a blood test. Afterwards, the doctor was concerned about the high alcohol level in my blood so early in the morning. He ordered me to report to a treatment facility and told me that if I refused, I would be fired. I didn't understand what the fuss was about because I didn't see myself as an alcoholic, just a heavy drinker.

During the nineteen days I spent in the facility, I kept to myself and continued my denial. Two of my friends, who were British, came to visit me and slipped me a vial of valium, which helped me immensely with the telltale "shakes" of an alcoholic. The treatment staff knew nothing about my having these pills or that I was popping them periodically. Since we were allowed to go out on passes, I even managed to locate some marijuana to smoke. This also took the edge off and certainly kept me from appearing too jumpy.

A few days after I was discharged, my husband found me in our closet, sitting in my suitcase, crying hysterically while trying to comb my long hair, which was a snarled mess. Keith took me to a psychiatric hospital and had me admitted immediately. It took several days for me to come out of what seemed to be a trance. The psychiatrist, who ministered to me, tried to find out why I was so emotionally ill. He thought that my emotional struggles probably were a result of my father's continual negative influence. Our relationship had been a strained one. My father had been a mystery to everyone, especially to me.

Prologue

In the beginning, when I had a few months of sobriety, Elynore O'Bryan, I my sponsor, asked me to write my story as part of the healing journey A. connected with the Twelve-step Program. I wasn't hopeful about being able to tell it all for her. It seemed like a huge, complicated and impossible assignment. I persevered, however, and it got done. It saddens me char Elynore didn't live long enough to read it.

My story is one of courage, faith and survival. Despite my bipolar mental disorder, which caused at least five accepts at suicide, and my self-medication with alcohol, I dared to hope that somehow, someday, my life would eventually get better.

The New Testament in the Bible tells us, "The birds of the air don't worry because their Heavenly Father provides for them." Despite my wayward lifestyle during my drinking years, I was fed daily. Admittedly, sometimes I got fed at the eleventh hour, bur I have managed to get fed in the most amazing ways, continuously to this day. Daily, I ask to be provided for physically, mentally and spiritually—**just for today.**

People have asked me why I believe in God and I tell them I believe in Him because I believe in His miracles. If you ask me why I would believe this way, then I will tell you it is because I have seen God perform a miracle for me in my life.

I had the privilege of attending a women's weekend religious retreat called Via de Cristo, while my husband attended one for men. We both attended the Via de Cristo reunion and were delighted to have Rev. Joseph Girzone, author of *Joshua,* as our speaker. He told us a story about the apostle John, who took care of Jesus' mother, Mary, after the crucifixion of Jesus. One day when John was very old, blind and barely able to walk, his friends asked him to tell them about Jesus. John replied, "Love one another."

His friends persisted, "No, tell us about what Jesus caught."

John replied again, "Love one another."

Agitated, the people asked again, "No, tell us what Jesus said to you!"

John patiently replied, "Love one another."

Love is patient and kind. Love is not jealous or boastful or proud or rude. Love does not demand its own way. love is not irritable, and it keeps no record of when it has been wronged. It is never glad about injustice but rejoices whenever the truth wins out. Love never gives up, never loses faith, is always hopeful, and endures through every circumstance.

Love will last forever, but prophecy, speaking in unknown languages, and special knowledge will all disappear. Now we know only a little and the gift of prophecy reveals little! But when the end comes, these special gifts will all disappear.

It's like this: When I was a child, I spoke and thought and reasoned as a child does. But when I grew up, I put away childish things. Now we see things imperfectly, as in a poor mirror, but then we will see everything with perfect clarity. All that I know now is partial and incomplete, but then I will know everything completely, just as God knows me now.

*There are three things that will endure-faith, hope and love-and the greatest of these is love. **1 Corinthians 13:4-13***

1

Beginnings

While I was fighting my jet lag, I sleepily gazed out the airport bus window as we skirted the exotic white beaches of Phuket, Thailand. I was excited about the reality of finally sailing aboard chis historically accurate rail ship in the waters of the Andaman Sea. I was exhausted from the twenty-four-hour flight across the Pacific. J hadn't been able to sleep for any length of time on the plane, and it crossed my mind that taking this exotic cruise might not have been that great an idea after all. All I could think about was how great it would feel to crawl into my bunk and know the bliss of sleep.

Then, on the horizon I saw the Star Flyer and she took my breath away. She was regal, proud and even more a true sailing ship than I had imagined. My fatigue instantly vanished; all I could think of was being aboard and underway in a matter of hours.

My excitement would have to wait-there were over a hundred passengers to be organized, luggage to be sorted, passports to be handed to the tour guide, groups to be formed and the ship's launches to board.

Not realizing the tour guide was inexperienced in tour coordination, passengers were irritable and irate, besides we were all half-dead from jet lag.

By the time we were all seeded in the launches with our maces and our carry-on luggage, all was quiet in anticipation of our dreams becoming a genuine reality. The ship was such an amazing sight as we approached that some of us had tears in our eyes. The Star Flyer had elegant classic lines; her paint work and varnish sparkled as did the polished brass. That my dream of someday sailing on a tall ship, was now a reality flabbergasted me.

I was numb as one of the crew members offered me his hand to step out of the launch and onto the ship's gangway. From there it was up to me to climb the long staircase chat rose along the side of the ship to the main deck. It was a long way to go and my legs felt like rubber.

I was unprepared for the sight of the beautiful and tiny, elegant Thai woman who stood in front of me when I reached the main deck. Dressed in the native ornate costume of brilliantly colored silk in pinks, oranges, royal blues and yellows and trimmed in gold. She had a golden pointed crown on her head and she bowed and smiled at each of us in such a render and sincere war I was moved to tears. Next to her stood the captain, a bear of a man dressed in a crisp, bright white officers uniform, who saluted and welcomed us aboard ship. Stewards showed us to our staterooms as the efficient crew prepared the ship to get underway.

Once underway, we returned to the main deck to watch and cake it all in. The sun was setting as the square-rigged sailing vessel eased out of the harbor. The jibs were set and the square-rigged sails unfurled electronically while we listened to the strains of classical Norwegian seagoing music sung by a men's choir, whose deep and rhythmical voices created an ethereal magical moment for all onboard. Russian and Ukrainian officers on the bridge stood erect and serene in their flawless white uniforms as the ship's 36,000 square feet of majestic sails filled up with the might of the wind. We felt the intensity of the ship's power as she starred to move rapidly through the indigo waters and in to the sunset.

My husband and I stood at the railing gazing at the sea and the setting sun, feeling the wind all around us. We were bound for the Similan Islands, the Andaman Sea and many exotic pores before reaching our final destination Singapore.

As I watched the sunset, my past years began to flood my mind. I thought back in time as I watched the glorious pink, coral and gold multihued sky dip slowly into the indigo sea.

I was so deep in thought; I didn't hear my husband say he was going below to unpack.

My thoughts wandered back to my beginning.

Born in the Hawaiian Islands 1946, I was known as a Kanaki, Hawaiian for "white woman born in the Islands." At that point in rime, Hawaii was only a territory of the United Scares.

My father was a Naval Officer, call, strong and handsome. I was just five days old when my father first took me into the sea with him. Due to my mother's fear of water, he was the one I bonded with from infancy onwards. The memories of chose days have stayed with me through the years. I remember the look of approval and love he gave me because I was not afraid when he swung me through the waves, he got me to squeal and giggle with delight. I felt the strength and comfort of his arms as he protected me from the surging ocean around us. The flower-scented breeze, mixed with his aftershave and the warm water, caused an indelible memory, my version of perfect happiness, my emotional nirvana and the food of my soul. Perhaps as a result, I have spent much of my life seeking the couch of a man.

When a tsunami took out half the island of Oahu just before we left Hawaii, Father Val persuaded my parents to christen me. My father chose the name Jon, a tradition in his family, and added Susan because the Black-eyed Susan, which grew in the Blue Ridge Mountains, was his favorite flower. Thus I became "Jon Susan."

As the sails billowed and the ship groaned ever so slightly, I was truly aware of the meaning of the AA slogan, "Don't give up before the miracle." This sailing opportunity was, without a doubt, a miracle. I was aboard the ship of my dreams, ready for an exhilarating and amazing experience. I had come so far from the depths of drunken despair, loneliness, poverty and the disease of manic-depression, bipolar disorder.

Alcohol had beaten and defeated me and it was complicated by the manic- depression. All I had had to do to reach chis moment was not to drink, to take just one day at a time. The days had added up slowly, bur before I knew it, small miracles had begun to happen in my life.

My dictatorial and abusive father demanded that my mother and I obey his orders. His behavior affected my relationships with men throughout my life. Never having developed the ability to handle confrontation, I became a woman who would go to any length to please a man. Before I knew about sex, I was exceptionally poised and an attentive listener. When I discovered the delights of sex, I became increasingly popular. Powerful men were drawn to me because they found me exceptionally feminine and cooperative. Once in a relationship, I became totally consumed by the man and lost my identity, becoming submissive and totally dependent. It became a habit that continues today.

When I discovered drinking, I used it as a means of easing my emotional discomfort and fear of intimacy. Bur everything backfired and my life went downhill. Alcohol brought on the cunningly slow progression of the madness of manic-depression-bipolar disorder, which is often associated with alcohol abuse. Mixing my rampant promiscuity with the onset of manic-depression and excessive consumption of alcohol produced a lifetime of dramatic chaos and continuous disappointment. It took twenty long difficult years of therapy, countless mental instructions and the deep faith I eventually found in my Higher Power, through the help of the Twelve-step Program, to curtail this insanity and bring my life to some semblance of control.

After all the years of pain, I am now able to express in writing some of my important life experiences. I finally felt the bliss of the freedom to express myself and share my story with you. My journey has been a difficult, tiresome and sometimes discouraging one, but I did rake the "scenic route." The drinking didn't just happen by itself. I inherited the disease from both my parents. I am immensely grateful to be a recovering woman in a Twelvestep Program. I feel like I have trekked up an extremely steep slippery slope, yet survived to experience a miraculous lifestyle and the continuation of more adventure.

By now the sun was gone and the darkness revealed the clarity of the starlit sky. I was deep in thought until my husband came to my side and slipped his arm around my shoulders and pointed out the Southern Cross for me. The magnificent sky was absolutely brilliant with scars. I felt I was where I belonged because I had always needed the touch of a man who shared my love of travel and adventure. My father had cold me early in my life the importance of companionship when sharing adventures.

We moved to Washington, O.C., where my father attended George Washington University to study fine art. He turned the third floor of our house into his arc studio and became an accomplished artist. Bur it was my mother who spent hours with me showing me how to hold the crayons and stay within the lines of the coloring books. Their artistic taste was different; she loved brilliant colors while my fathers color choices tended to be somewhat somber. Although I loved the talented art of each, I eventually preferred vibrant colors. Both of my parents competed for my attention. My mother was a sensitive Southern lady with a nursing degree bur no formal artistic education, yet she could paint and draw beautifully. Since she wasn't strong enough to accept my fathers criticism, it was rare chat she would do anything artistic on her own.

My father asserted his superiority in the marriage by flaunting his degree in both landscape architecture and engineering from Penn Scare, not to mention his horticultural studies at Harvard. On weekends he would paint watercolors in Foggy Bottom, the old neighborhood where he was born and grew up. That funky old section of the city was torn down years ago to create the huge Watergate development, which became famous in Nixons day.

While my father was out painting, my mother spent the rime showing me how to draw, cutting out paper dolls and helping me with the scissors, pencils or crayons. I seem to learn best visually and since my mother was very patient and render when she was sober, I thrived artistically when I was young and receiving all of her undivided attention.

Most of my rime in chose early years was spent with my mother or grandmother.

In spite of their education and accomplishments, my parents had only a few things in common: they loved to travel, to cell jokes and laugh. They also had a passion for eating out in small, bistro-type restaurants, mostly Italian and Greek and owned by friends of my fathers, where they would drink to excess and then argue. My mother was not a good cook and wasn't comfortable in the kitchen. As my father put it, "Anything is better than Kacie's cooking." My parents took me with them, and many of my early nighttime memories are of falling asleep in restaurant highchairs.

Rarely do I remember them chinking alike on anything—except when my mother was sober. When she wasn't drinking, she was timid and submissive around my father, yet had a wonderful sense of humor. After one or two drinks, she became overly affectionate, wanting to be everyone's friend, and slowly became more and more grandiose. As she continued to drink, her personality changed significantly and she turned into a cold, sarcastic, and antagonistic woman.

Even at a very early age, I could feel the tension build when my parents drank. Because of their personality and mood changes during those rimes, I didn't know how to relate to either of chem. They were polar opposites, always pulling me in two different directions.

When I was very small, I was afraid of my father and avoided him when he was drunk, because he angered easily and considered me a nuisance. When I was older and able to communicate with him, he seemed charmed by my believing everything he told me. He would make up stories to tell me and take the time to read to me from children's books. To please him, I had to be quiet and very careful to listen attentively to everything he said. Although he might have resented me at my birth, by the time I was about three or four, he treated me gently and seemed delighted with having a daughter.

My domineering father made a significant impact upon my life and affected my romantic choice of men during my younger years of womanhood. As a perfectionist and a driven man, he was hard on me at times, obsessing on my being perfect and pushing me to succeed at every opportunity. My father was athletic, very active and gregarious. My shy and withdrawn mother did not have the energy, stamina or the enthusiasm for life my father and I possessed. Bur when she drank, it gave her a false sense of courage and energy to go into combat with my father and eventually with me.

It could be quiet at home until the drinking starred. As early as age four, I realized my home would be filled with insane drama on Friday nights and weekends, when my parents drank to excess. During happy hour at restaurant, my father had been known to polish off seven martinis, one after another, and char was before the meal. One of my earliest memories was watching my father, in a drunken rage, hurl a crystal ashtray into the mirrored door where my mother stood holding me. Shards of glass flew everywhere, splitting apart the mirrored door like an explosion. After the glass serried, all I could hear was the loud sounds of my father's yelling and my mother's sobs and screams. I rarely felt safe when my parents drink, and to this day I feel anxious around loud, confrontational people. I learned at an early age to detach and create my own world because the world of my parents was too insane and unstable. They appeared to thrive on the chaos and the confusion their drinking created.

Nannie, my father's mother, was the only person in my childhood I felt safe with. She gave me unconditional love and demonstrated it by hugging me; she spent as much time as she could spoiling me and patiently explaining things I didn't understand. In her eyes, her granddaughter could do no wrong, and I was her favorite person. Except for Roger and me, Nannie thought her family was composed of useless simpletons.

Helen Franklin Nebel, or Nannie, was an awesome character. She had inherited money but did not flaunt it, choosing instead to live in a modest house with her husband, Jon Frank, and Roger, a boarder who happened to also be her longtime lover. Petite with auburn hair, Nannie was not afraid of anyone or anything. In her younger days, family legend had it that she had beaten Presidents Harding and Coolidge at golf. One of her hobbies was raising bulldogs.

Roger, the boarder, was an attractive and wealthy, retired chemist who had joined the household when my father was four years old. Nannie was fed up with her husband, who she referred to as an idiot. My carefree, happy grandfather spent most of his time at the racetrack, or at his favorite bar, always smoking his cigars and being rather jovial about everything. Nannie was attracted to the brilliant Roger and since her husband wouldn't initiate a divorce, she took up with her boarder and the living situation remained the same until she died. Although Roger was cantankerous and impatient with noisy, inquisitive children, he was generous with his money toward my mother and me.

This living situation had to have caused a great deal of emotional confusion for my father. I'm sure that he didn't know how to accept his mother's lifestyle. However, no one in the family seemed overly concerned with the lover being an addition to the family, perhaps because each of the three adults had their own bedroom. My grandmother was very strong-willed and no one approached her on this subject or ochers chat might make her angry. After all, she was the one controlling the purse strings, and my parents and my grandfather were not willing to upset their financial security.

Because permanent chaos was a part of my parents' lives, my grandmother was constantly designated to settle their arguments. Not only did she think they were idiots the way they lived and acted, she was also concerned with the money they were spending by eating out, especially because she was frugal. Being alcoholics in denial, my parents resented Nannie's interference.

Despite earning a good living, my father was stingy and right with money and there was always discord between my parents when it came to finances. Coming from a large, poor family, my mother was greedy and delighted in the opportunity to spend money. She would be as nice as she could to Nannie, hoping Nannie would loosen her purse strings and rake my mother shopping. I could cell that Nannie had very little use for my mother. My grandmother, critical of my mothers small town upbringing, would sometimes refer to my mother as a hick. Years later, my mother cold me that it was impossible for her to please her mother-in-law.

I was the apple of my grandmothers eye; Nannie was always generous when it came to me. In her eyes I was an adorable child with a sweet and loving disposition. But she didn't wait to see how I would turn out, she enrolled me in the preschool program at the prestigious Holy Cross Academy when I was born to make sure I got a good start with my education. In anticipation of the future, she even bought me a complete set of sterling silver flatware to use when r got married. Knowing how benevolent she was with me, my father went to her for my financial needs.

In her will, my grandmother left a dollar to my father, her only child. She left a life estate to her survivors (her husband, Roger, and my parents), which gave them the right to live in her house until they died. Her will left me the ownership of her house and all her money.

My grandmother had her first stroke when she was sixty-four and I was about four years old. In those days, children were not permitted inside the hospital. I remember my father taking me to the hospital grounds; when he pointed to a window, I could see Roger helping Nannie wave to me. After what seemed to me like a very long time, she was finally released from the hospital. When she came home restricted to a wheelchair, I could see and feel the fear and desperation in my grandmother's eyes. Once such a beautiful and active woman, she could no longer speak and was a prisoner of her wheelchair for the rest of her life, just when we all needed her leadership, her spunk, and her courage.

Two years later, when I was six, my parents planned to move to Europe. Both my parents loved to travel; it was one of the positive parts of their relationship. As I grew up, I found I had inherited this gypsy spirit.

Nannie had always been aware of my father's whims to take off and move on, but I can only imagine my grandmother's pain over this desertion. I was six and still spending many nights falling asleep in restaurant booths while my parents drank and argued. With my Nannies affliction and my parents vagabond ways, I lost the last stable influence in my young life, and my grandmother lost the company of her beloved granddaughter.

2

An International Citizen

Our move to Europe in 1952 was made possible by the art fellowship my father had won to attend the Bellas Artes in Madrid, Spain. We sailed to Europe aboard the French cruising ship *La Liberte* and disembarked at Le Havre, a port on the west coast of France. With our huge mound of luggage, we went by train to Paris.

When we arrived by taxi at our Parisian hotel, my father grumbled about the expensive taxi fare. Money was always an issue with my father. "Take the luggage into the lobby," he ordered the driver.

"Merde, it is not my job, just pay me for the journey," the Frenchman said, shrugging his shoulders.

Having had too much wine on the train, my father slugged the taxi driver. My father had had a pretty remarkable career as an amateur boxer in both high school and at Penn State. He told me he had once fought Jack Dempsey. Even though my father had gotten the dickens kicked out of him, he was pretty proud to have had the opportunity to be in the ring with such a well-known boxer.

"You communist!" the driver shouted as he fought back. He was no match for my father, even in his inebriated state, and the driver came out the loser. The gendarmes were called and it took at least two hours to sort out the mess. I didn't care who won or lost this fight; I was beside myself with embarrassment and confused by the violence and hostility my father seemed to cause.

As we unpacked and seeded into our rooms, my father commented, "I believe we've rented rooms in a bordello."

"Why, have you seen any questionable women lurking about, Frank?" my mother ceased.

"This place is so rundown. Didn't you notice all the people corning and going in the hallway?"

"Let's just make the best of it," she replied as she continued to explore. "By the way, why is there such a small hole in the toilet?"

"Don't you know what that is, Kacie?" my father asked as he laughed at her.

"I wouldn't have asked if I knew for sure. How can we pee in it?" she asked as she anticipated his putdown.

"I guess you never saw a bidet in Virginia, did you? The French use chis after lovemaking." My mother was embarrassed at her ignorance and cried to laugh it off.

Although we were in Paris only briefly before we cook a train to Madrid, it gave me just enough rime to register some childish impressions of an exciting and colorful city. I delighted in the busy streets filled with animated people, tiny cars and outdoor cafes. I still remember the delicious smell of freshly baked bread.

In Madrid, our home was a penthouse with a lovely terrace char overlooked the red tiled rooftops of the city and allowed us plenty of Spanish sunshine. For inexplicable Spanish reasons, the elevator operated only at night. Since shops were only open during the day, we had to carry everything upstairs by hand. I felt particularly sympathetic for the iceman, who arrived regularly every morning with a huge block for our icebox, since we didn't have a refrigerator. After seven flights of stairs, sweating and straining the whole way, he was ready for the cool drink offered by friendly Pepita, our happy, fat maid. He relaxed in a chair and chatted a while before he went on to his next customer.

I was fascinated with Spain during the 1950's. Because the dictator Franco was in power, there was no crime. We quickly acclimated to Spanish ways and would go our lace for a meal, which is common in Spain. When we returned to the front of our apartment building, often after midnight, my father would clap his hands loudly. A gentleman in a long dark cape would whirl around the corner carrying a huge ring char held all the keys to the ornate iron gates of the apartments in our neighborhood. I remember the jingling sound of the keys and the rushing footsteps as he approached us to open our gate. My parents were usually jovial and not overly drunk because we had had a late siesta before our meal

Getting into the tiny, antique wrought iron elevator was always a challenge. We never knew if it would scare at all, and couldn't help but wonder if the elevator would continue to rise once it did get going. The contraption clattered and groaned all the way up to our top floor. My mother often suggested skipping the elevator, but my father and I always wanted to gamble on whether we could make the thing work its way up. I looked forward to the elevator adventure every time we ate out.

I resonated with the slow Spanish pace of life, taking it easy was acceptable in Spain. I was not expected to act quickly or recklessly, and life was only as complicated as you made it out to be. I w:is expected to be gentle and to take my time and soon began to forget the pressured and hurried American ways. It seemed to me then that everything in America was concerned with speed.

We didn't need an alarm clock, in the mornings we were awakened by the braying of donkeys, as they towed the gypsies' carts that came to pick up our crash every morning like clockwork. There were vehicles on the streets, but even they were different and old-fashioned. When we took a taxi, the driver started the vehicle by turning a crank up in the front. That made sense to me then because most toys had to be wound up in order to operate.

The move to Spain might have been a deliberate attempt by my parents to get away from Nannie's eagle eye and her constant attempts to control our lives, but she didn't forget her granddaughter. She wanted me to receive a proper upbringing, regardless of where I lived. I believe if my grandmother could have communicated with me, she would have told me she was doing her best to keep me in one place long enough for me to become accustomed to my surroundings. Since she couldn't do anything about my parents' nightly debauchery, she could do something for my schooling. To give me some structure and stability in my life, Nannie sent the tuition for *Santa Teresa de Jesus,* a Catholic boarding school in Madrid.

My parents were probably relieved to know I was safely tucked away in school and they were provided with freedom to do as they pleased.

Having been in a Catholic pre-school since I was three years old, I was familiar with nuns running my life. After the chaos of my parents' lifestyle, Spanish boarding school was a haven of peacefulness and structured routine. I shared a room with two little girls in the Babies' Ward. For privacy and modesty, each bed was surrounded by white curtains, a concept we didn't grasp as children. Modesty is not something children worry about by nature. We thought the curtains were an attempt to keep us from playing, acting silly and being noisy, as noise was something char was *never* tolerated. The nuns made every attempt to keep us silent, but we learned how to read each others eyes and hearts.

It wasn't unusual to receive a mighty chump on the head now and then for misbehaving or talking when we were supposed to be silent, but there were more loving hugs than thumps by the end of the day. The nuns who crossed my path during my elementary education were very loving and their love was unconditional. The peace and serenity was a welcome contrast to my parents' violent unpredictability. Now, I realize I am one of the fortunate Roman Catholics who has fond memories of the nuns. The nuns taught us to write script beautifully before they taught us how to print, and the care they gave us was always one-on-one. One of the nuns, who was very loving and patient with me, spend many hours trying to teach me how to memorize poems and lessons. By the time I was nine, I could paint and draw well. We were taught to speak French and to play the piano. I eventually forgot about English and began to think in Spanish.

Parents were allowed to visit every Sunday, and to take us out for the day every other Sunday. As it is with most young children, foreign languages came easily to me, and I became fluent in Spanish. When we ate out, we would usually go to a local restaurant near the school, where my father would proudly have me order the meal in Spanish. My father would shower me with affection and called me his "Little Senorita," which had to be painful for my mother. Slowly I watched her withdraw and become more and more jealous of me.

My mother had lost her father just before Christmas when she was only ten years old, and her mother was left with seven small children to raise alone. My mother never got over her loss. I think my mother had been looking for a further figure in her husband to replace the father whom she claimed had adored her. Looking back, I'm sure her jealous feelings had very little to do with me. Later on in life, I discovered my parents had been unfaithful to each other since the beginning of their marriage and continued chis behavior while we were in Europe. I don't think my mother was a very happy person, and I found myself withdrawing from her as well. Most of my focus revolved around my father by then; I wanted to make him happy and win his approval. My mother was just too distant to reach.

The nuns taught me important lessons chat would stick with me the rest of my life. One valuable lesson was about vanity. Every morning two nuns were assigned to me, one to dress me in my pinafore, the other to braid my long hair. Eventually, they decided to cut off my braids so only one sister would be needed to dress me.

My father came to visit shortly afterward. "What have you done to my daughters beautiful hair?" he asked, crying to control his anger because he was furious. "I am nor pleased. She was such a pretty girl, and now she looks like some street urchin! This is definitely not how I want her to look!"

"This will be good in the long run for your daughter," one of the nuns patiently explained, silencing my fathers protests. He wouldn't dare fight with a nun.

The new haircut really didn't bother me, but I was definitely not a pretty sight. I was petite, rather skinny and had prominent eyes, so I looked somewhat like a cricket. My hair had little or nothing to do with my playing with the other girls, my art, or my piano lessons, but it remained an irritation to my father, and he resented it for our remaining days in Spain. My father's disappointment in the nuns cutting my hair must have impacted me because I've worn my hair long for most of my life.

Another lesson was about sharing and equality. There were no cliques at chis school; girls of every age intermingled. I learned not to snub anyone or to feel superior, unlike my parents, who had tremendous, egos and felt superior to most people. I'm sure they even felt superior to me. When my grandmother sent me gifts of new dresses, I had to wear them under my white brocade pinafore so as not to stand out from the other children.

When she sent me dolls, I was only allowed to play with them on Sunday, and only if I shared them with my classmates. This broke my heart ac the time. I was very attached to my dolls, especially my "Tiny Tears." They were the only things I had control over in my life, the only way I could construct a world of my own where things were orderly and everyone behaved. I played with dolls up to the age of thirteen, and stopped then only because it became embarrassing. No one else at chat age seemed interested in dolls, but I gave them up sorrowfully.

Often du ring my days in Spain, I felt like a doll myself. I was a Strange little skinny child dragged hither and yon by two even stranger (usually intoxicated) adults, who claimed to be from either the United States or Canada, depending on my father's mood. I spoke the Spanish language well and I appeared normal, maybe even Spanish. Perhaps I was hoping that I did appear Spanish and not related to these two characters. My mother was always argumentative and antagonistic, especially if she had had too much wine. My parents demonstrated bizarre family dynamics, which were probably intriguing to some observers.

My father cold me not to tell anyone that I was a United States citizen. He wanted me to think of myself as an international citizen and for me to believe I belonged anywhere I wanted to belong in this world. He wanted me to feel at home and secure everywhere I went. He had started traveling even before college. While attending Penn State, he worked in a hotel in Bermuda during the summers and he emphasized that I should think about working abroad when I grew up. I was so young when I left America that I honestly began to forget about where I came from. Spain was so alive with her music, passion, charm and unique flavor. To me, Spain even had her own smell-it was delicious!

The nuns did not allow us to see movies, but my father wanted to take me to see "Peter Pan" and asked me to keep it a secret from the nuns. It made such an impression on me that from then on I made it a habit of cracking the window open each night. There was always the chance char Peter Pan would come during the night and teach me how to Ay. Since the first movie was so much fun, we also went to see "Pollyanna." Toudled by the fact char Pollyanna in the movie carries a special locker from her deceased father, my father gave me an identical locket. I still have it to remind me of a happy experience with my dad.

Just when I'd gotten to feel completely at home in Spain, we moved again. We went to live in Bar-le-Due, a small French village about one hundred miles east of Paris. We had to give up trying to live on the sale of my father's artwork and the money chat Nannie sent us.

"We're living in a cow town, Katie," my father would joke with my mother. "All I ever see are cows all around us. And we're nor even in Texas."

While living there, my father would go away for no apparent reason and never mention why he left. It's still a mystery to me, but many years later, someone pointed out that it was obvious my father had been working for Naval Intelligence. What I did know was that he worked as a civil engineer for the Army Corps of Engineers. He was helping to design and build a helicopter pad in an ammunition depot within a small U.S. Army base. I'm sure there was far more to his job, but that was all I was told.

In Bar-le-Due, I attended a French Catholic girls' school as a day student. An Irish nun cried to tutor me in English and attempted to reach me how to knit and do other needlework. I was a total disaster at knitting, but chis nun remained very patient as if there were a possibility I would catch on eventually. English was also difficult for me and though I struggled, she was unsuccessful at reaching me to read it. In those days, very little was known about reading disorders, such as dyslexia, and mine was ignored for most of my education both in Europe and in the United States.

We lived in a small hotel, and I had my own room where I played alone with my dolls. I was very happy with the bathroom bidet, which I considered my dolls' very own bathtub. When my father gave me a large lump of clay to play with, I happily made all kinds of make-believe cakes and pastries to serve at my tea parries for my dolls.

Eventually, I made friends with two English girls and we are dinner by ourselves in the hotel dining room early in the evening. Our parents ate much lacer. My father often complained about the rich French sauces since he liked much plainer food. He enjoyed Oriental cooking and Greek cuisine, nowhere to be found in rural France in the '50's. He wasn't happy with the French attitude either; he felt they acted high and mighty!

I knew nothing about bigotry and racism, especially as it concerned my father. One day a black U.S. Army serviceman brought his little boy to my door; he was looking for a playmate for his son. "Would you like this comic book?" the friendly little boy asked when I opened the door.

"My daughter is not interested in your comic book," my father said, suddenly appearing at my door. "I want you to leave, please," he said curtly.

I saw the deep hurt and rejection registering in the eyes of the father and son, but I could hardly believe the hatred and hostility in my father's eyes. Puzzled, I couldn't stop looking at him.

"You won't understand this now, Joni, but Negroes are nor our kind of people. We moved to Europe to get away from them," he explained. It contradicted what he had told me about becoming an international citizen. How could I belong everywhere if some people were considered unacceptable?

Life in France w:is very quiet, especially when my father was traveling. I would spend some of those nights in my parents- room with my mother. Sometimes she would cuddle me and tell me how much I meant to her and how much I loved me, other times she would chase me and threaten to hit me. We had a "slap-kiss" relationship. Consequently, I learned to keep my emotions to myself and had no expectations of her or my father. I never learned how to trust or when the other shoe would fall. It led me to live in a perpetual state of fear and to be more and more anxious as I grew up.

One day a red-haired woman knocked on my hotel door. This stranger was wearing a sheer, see-through nightgown. "Would you like to come to my room and see my hamsters?" she asked in a British accent.

"Sure," I said. I was nine years old and alone in my hotel room. Even though I thought she was oddly dressed for daytime, I followed her down the hall. Suddenly, a man jumped out into the hallway with a knife. Then my father appeared. Someone threw my father a bottle, he broke it and the two men scarred for each other. I just stood there transfixed with this strange woman.

Moments later, my mother came running out of her room. "Stop!" she yelled as she jumped between the two men. Amazingly, they stopped. Everyone returned to their rooms, hue I remained standing there alone, seemingly forgotten.

"Mon cher, do not worry," one of the chambermaids, who had been watching, said gently as she led me back to my room "What is the name of your doll, little girl?" she asked as she picked up one of my dolls. I was quiet since I was ashamed for the way my parents acted, and I was hurt because they hadn't shown any concern for me. I seemed of no consequence to them, almost as if I were invisible. About this time I began to notice chat my parents' most outlandish behavior patterns went hand in hand with the smell of French wine.

About a year later when we moved to Frankfurt, Germany, my life got worse. My father continued working as a civil engineer. I was enrolled in a coed English-speaking school for the first time since we left the United States. I was mortified to be going to school with boys. Since I had a great deal of difficulty reading and understanding English, I was placed two grades behind so I was older than my classmates and felt stupid. My shame was almost incapacitating, but there was so much I could not understand about my whole life at this time. I had absolutely no one I felt I could crust or confide in. I was becoming more and more aware of my parents' consumption of alcohol and realizing how powerless I was to do anything about it.

In Spain and France, they had drunk wine, brandies and cognac. Now in Germany, beer was added to their diet. I only noticed chis because it seemed the more they drank, the louder and more demonstrative their arguments became. We ace out almost every evening and when my parents would argue openly and loudly, threaten each other, and shout insults and obscenities, I wanted to hide under the cable and pretend they weren't my parents.

Father would always flirt with a young and pretty waitress, which irritated my mother. "Frank, you're such an idiot and an egotist," Mother would say to retaliate.

"Go shit in your hat," he'd reply to antagonize her further, and then he'd make his flirting even more obvious. The waitresses were usually flirtatious since they knew Americans would tip, and besides, my father was good looking.

Their arguing in public was extremely embarrassing for me; I lost respect for them and hated to be seen with chem. I thought they were disgusting, especially when they were noticeably drunk and stumbling around.

The best part of our European years was the weekend trips we cook when my father could get a few days off My artistic parents, especially my father, delighted in art museums and we must have visited all of the important ones throughout Europe during chose years. Generally, my parents were better behaved during chose weekend jaunts. Perhaps it helped them forget about their own misery with each other.

I was greatly relieved when I found out we were returning to the United States in 1959. The German language had been difficult for me; I was having enough problems crying to learn to read English. I found the pronunciation and the German grammar to be impossible to comprehend.

My father decided we needed to go home because he was concerned about his mother's health. Nannie was getting progressively worse with each stroke. So far she had had six strokes and each time it was a miracle she had lived through it. I chink Dad sensed that this time his mother would die. He finally acted guilty about his inattention to her and her needs. I was pretty excited to be leaving Europe and to be going home to see my Nannie again. But I knew my mother would miss the European attitude-chat it was an accepted fact of life to drink all day!

We came home in 1959 on a U.S. military ship, USNS Patch, from Bremerhaven. My fathers rank as a lieutenant commander provided us a choice cabin. One of the funniest memories of my life took place in our cabin one night during a terrible storm. Our experiences abroad were summed up by chis incident. My mother had gotten up in the dark and had accidentally stepped into one of the drawers that had come open from under her bunk. She was stuck in the drawer, which was now loose and sliding madly around the room, as if she were on a surfboard! Her screams awakened us and brought in a military policeman, who was on duty outside in the corridor. He rescued my mother, and we all laughed hysterically, the first time I could remember us all laughing together.

My mothers plight so aptly portrayed the family dynamic of sliding all over, out of control, panicked and screaming, wishing someone would rescue us. It was obvious to me at chat time how much contrast there was in my family. My grandmother had had the strength to manage my parents, but once they'd left her, their lives in Europe had become unmanageable.

When we came home I was a teenager. Because of my grandmother's generosity in sending me to boarding schools in Europe, I had at lease known a small sense of security. I was beginning to realize how adversely alcohol affected my parents' behavior. Ac chat time I could not know the extent to which my early life would also affect me in the future, and how it would shape my adult life.

3

Nazareth

My grandmother continued to get worse. She had had her seventh stroke by the time we reached Washington, O.C., and she was struggling with her impending death. My mother, being a registered nurse, took on the job of private duty nurse for Nannie.

On the July 4th holiday, my father was planning to cake me to the beach. Before we left, my mother called to tell him my grandmother was dying and asked us to stop by the hospital. Different doctors had told us several times in the past that Nannie wasn't going to make it, but it was a shock to be cold she was truly dying this time. In her room I stood by her hospital bed and could hear the death rattle coming from Nannie's throat. I watched my grandmother watching me while she died, wondering what I should say or feel. I didn't know what to believe about death. It was too terrible to believe that I would never see her alive again, not ever. My heart was broken, but all I could do was to look into her eyes and wonder where she was going.

My mother and father were crying, but I didn't understand why since neither of them had ever seen eye to eye on *anything*. Now they were much more emotional than I had ever been. All of my life my mother stopped me when I got close w being emotional; she'd say, "Stop emoting because it's unacceptable behavior."

When it was obvious Nannie had died, the doctor somberly turned to my father, "Mr. Nebel, your wife has just died."

"I'm sorry, doctor, but she was my mother," my father added softly.

My tall handsome father was not at all insulted because Nannie didn't look even close to her age of seventy-two. She still had flawless skin and long beautiful hair with almost no gray in it. It was amazing for me to see Nannie lying there so still and lifeless. She appeared so lovely and finally looked at peace. Nannie had been one of the only people in my life who had loved me unconditionally, and had never been judgmental of me in the way my parents were. I was relieved to know that, after all the many years of not being able to speak or walk, my grandmother was finally a free spirit—literally!

Looking back, I realize I did not mourn my grandmothers death because I didn't know how. Neither of my parents seemed to know how either. At the funeral parlor my parents at first treated this incident like a festive social gathering. Then both of them straightened up and faced the issue soberly. When I went over to the coffin and touched my grandmother's hand, I was astounded that it felt like marble. No one had ever tried to explain the scientific intricacies of death to me. I knew the casket was only there to contain her body, because the Nannie I knew wasn't there anymore. Even then, as a fourteen-year-old, I believed my grandmother was with me at that moment, but not in the casket.

It took weeks for the reality to hit my father. When it did, he would lock himself in Nannie's room where he would weep for her for long periods of time. He locked the door when he came out and refused to lee anyone couch her belongings. Years went by, but her room remained untouched by everyone. Roger and my grandfather continued to live in Nannie's house. They had come together to help her through her years of disability, bur when she died they congenially led their separate lives.

———

When we came home because of Nannie's illness, my parents and I moved back into our Washington, D.C. home, which we had rented out while we were in Europe. I was sent to Sc. Mary's Academy, a Catholic boarding school for girls in nearby Maryland. At school I found a good friend in Linda, who also came from a troubled alcoholic home and had a *rageaholic* father. Linda and I shared a private alcove in a huge dormitory. We each had a single bed with a shelf and a cupboard at the head of the bed for our personal effects. Because we were both lonely, needy girls, we bonded almost immediately and became best friends. She was the first confidante I had ever had in my life, and we became like sisters.

Linda had eight brothers and sisters at home and seemed to me to be so serene and levelheaded about life. She was friendly with everyone in our class and very confident, where I was shy, frightened and preferred to keep my distance. Linda had a good sense of humor and gently poked fun at me and at my odd ways. I was clumsy, self-absorbed, socially awkward and too easily embarrassed. Because my father had forbidden me to ask him any personal questions, I grew up feeling I could not ask others about themselves and often wondered what I should divulge about myself. Should I keep everything a secret?

With Linda's help, I began to laugh at myself and I started to shake off my peculiarities and hang-ups. I went home with her often to her house right on a Chesapeake Bay beach in Maryland. I have wonderful memories of the merriment char resulted from a huge, happy family despite her parents' drinking. There were always friends, aunts and uncles around and lots of laughter. When I went to visit her in the warm months, we never got out of our bathing suits except to sleep. We swam and water-skied all day.

The school was divided scholastically between those who would attend college and chose who were advised to cake secretarial classes. Since my father envisioned me as a dentist or an architect, f was put in the college-oriented classes. Linda had no finances for college, so she was designated for the secretarial section. It was so ironic because Linda was brilliant and helped me with my homework while doing her own. I couldn't pass the Latin class and found many of the other classes to be difficult and close to impossible to understand.

Linda eventually overcame her financial challenges and years later, after raising a family, graduated with honors from Georgetown University. I have always thought that Linda's intelligence should have been enough to send her to college and her financial state should have been overlooked. In contrast, I've never graduated from any of the many colleges I attended, despite five years of study in colleges all over the United States.

———————◇———————

One Sunday, my mother paid me a surprise visit at St. Mary's. She was sober, dressed nicely in a navy blue suit and smelled softly sweet. Linda and I had been our walking and were delighted to see her because she rarely came to visit.

"Joni, I know this is a surprise, but I need your help. I'm planning to divorce your father and I need some money."

"Oh... " I said, only a little surprised. "How can I help with money?" My father had always handled all the finances and told me money and my financial worth were none of my business. His attitude caused me later to think of money in unrealistic terms. Even though I was to inherit Nannies estate at age twenty-one, I had not even considered what that might mean. My father was handling it, and that was fine with me.

"Well, I had to take some of your bonds out of your fathers safe deposit box. He doesn't know about it, of course. I need you to sign them over to me."

I felt pleased she was taking me into her confidence, and I had never thought about having the bonds in the first place. Since I was underage, I had no rights concerning them anyway. "OK, Mother. I'll do that for you."

"You know I'll be much happier on my own, Joni."

I fully agreed with her and noticed she seemed stronger and was full of purpose that day. Since she was a registered nurse, she was holding a good job in a hospital in Washington, D.C. and was still young enough to get on with her life.

The same evening my father came to visit, bringing me a huge basket of brilliant red apples. He told me he'd driven down from Penn State, where he had attended a football game. When I walked outside with him, even though it was dark I was pretty sure I saw a woman sitting in the front seat of his car. It was shocking to me, but it proved to me how right I was to give my mother the money. However, I felt torn between the two of them, and I felt I had betrayed my father. If my father knew I wanted this divorce, he would probably disown me and hate me.

When I came back into the dormitory, I went to my bed and couldn't stop crying. As my emotions got the better of me, I was put in the school's infirmary and was eventually diagnosed with a nervous breakdown.

Somehow, Linda helped me get through it. The other girls were kinder toward me and the nuns were very tender. Ironically, I had to almost lose my mind in order to be accepted and loved.

———————

The divorce case turned into a battle of accusations of poor character and affected who would receive custody of me. My mother hired a very expensive attorney for her divorce; his costs ate up most of my bonds. Since his security box lock was broken, my father proved my mother stole the bonds, and then he proved she was forging his checks. She struck back and proved with witnesses and employers that my father was a total mess and wasn't a fit parent either. The custody issue as confused and I was considered a ward of the court until it was settled.

I wasn't in the courtroom during the case, and because of my emotional pain, I've repressed most of the memories of that time. I do remember the judge had me come into his chambers privately to ask me which parent I would choose to live with.

"I don't think it's my place to choose," I told the judge frankly. "I'd rather you make that decision for me because I'm not ready to deal with any more guilt concerning my parents. I don't want to hurt either of them, and I wane to remain loyal to each of them, if possible."

The judge decreed that my father was financially responsible for me, an easy cask for him due to his position as trustee of my inheritance. The judge told him I was to attend boarding school and summer camp. I was to spend Christmas and Easter holidays with my father, and my mother would have me for the remaining holidays.

We were all affected emotionally by the divorce, and all three of us were on Valium. In the '60s, anyone whose life came unglued was put on the drug. I felt shame from the revelations about my parents that came out during the divorce case, and I was in a daze trying to cope with it. It was a relief to have it over, but I dealt with my feelings by caking more and more Valium and sleeping a lot. I never recovered from the guilt of knowing my money had caused so much bitterness and pain between my parents. I scarred to withdraw from people. I had to build my own wall around me to survive.

After the divorce, I was sent to a convent boarding school—Nazareth Academy in Nazareth, Kentucky, a few miles from Bardscown, Kentucky, where Stephen Foster wrote the song, "My Old Kentucky Horne." Nazareth was the oldest ladies' boarding school in the United States west of the Allegheny Mountains. The school name was in honor of the Sisters of Charity of Nazareth, nuns who were either nurses or teachers. It was famous during the Civil War for offering medical sanctuary to both Union and Confederate soldiers. Abraham Lincoln sent the nuns a thank you letter for providing this safe haven for both sides during the Civil War. The letter was posted on our bulletin board every year on Pres-ident's Day.

My father chose the school because of its excellent arc department. On its huge campus, dominated by the immense convene structure and its mini cathedral, there was a small stable of horses and an indoor swimming pool, and the school offered quite a number of activities for its students. I liked the looks of the school, with its acres of open land and beautiful trees and ponds.

During that time in the sixties there were many young women turning their lives over to God and entering the convent to become nuns, so it was a busy yet silent place. Just like in Spain, silence was the rule. I was able to make friends with the twenty girls in my class, but I was very careful to avoid any emotional intimacy. Ie just felt better to be on equal terms with everyone. Even though I was unhappy inside my own skin about my family issues, I was relieved to be in this peaceful and secure environment.

I met Leslie Morales my first day at Nazareth as a freshman. She was a beautiful upbeat redhead with sparkling green eyes and in the class ahead of me. We met in the smoking lounge in the activity building where the gym and swimming pool were located. Despite my young age, I was the only one in my class given permission to smoke. Because of my anxiety disorder, the doctor felt smoking might help me.

"Would you like to see the campus, get to know the lay of the land?" Leslie asked me with a smile after she had introduced herself.

'Sure," I said, not offering more about myself since I was still embarrassed about my parents. I didn't want any family secrets to disgrace me and keep me from being accepted.

"Let's go see the stables. You might like to go riding with me," she suggested.

We became friends and she eventually confided in me char she was the oldest in a family of ten children and her parents drank daily. I didn't feel totally alone making friends with someone whose home could have possibly been somewhat like mine. Leslie was bright and intelligent like Linda. Even though she had revealed some of her life, she kept her distance as well. It was a mutual thing, so no one's feelings got hurt.

In later years I attended some class reunions at Nazareth and realized we had *all* been in denial. We had needed to let our hurts and our feelings come to the surface, bur in those days we scuffed every emotion. The exterior had to be pristine.

During my sophomore year at Nazareth, my father moved to Costa Rica and my mother moved back to her hometown in the Blue Ridge Mountains of Virginia. I spent my summers at Camp Carriesbrook, an exclusive summer camp for women, which was located outside another small Virginia town. [learned horseback riding, proper cable manners and social graces. Because I had talent in art, I was privileged to teach sketching to some of the younger girls. I lost myself in learning to ride well and totally devoted myself to the task of teaching art. With boarding school, my art and the camp activities, my time was well spent. I was friendly enough, though not a close friend, with the ocher girls in my cabin and with the counselors. The girls in my cabin were all future debutantes, even though I wasn't in their social clique, they made me feel welcome and I didn't feel sad or lonely.

Once, that first summer at this camp, I visited my mother. She was staying at her mother's house in Virginia, recovering from recent surgery for cancer of the uterus. I was shocked that no one had informed me about her condition prior to my visit. Because of her rotten luck-receiving a divorce settlement from my father, losing custody of me and discovering she had cancer, all happening within one week-she had fallen into a deep depression. Withdrawn, tearful, weak, yet sober, she didn't have anything to say to me or to anyone else. Her behavior frightened me, making me feel she blamed me for the negative outcome of the divorce. I felt guilty because I was living a privileged life at summer camp and having fun while my mother suffered. That guile was a heavy burden for an awkward teenager, who was already too emotionally sensitive and high-strung. I began to use more Valium and withdrew even more within myself.

When I returned to Nazareth, knowing my mother was so sick and helpless worried me. She had her sister and her mother in Virginia, but I could tell during my visit that her mother and sister were withdrawn and resented Mother's drinking behavior. Over the years they had witnessed the dramatic change in my mother's personality when she drank. After a couple of drinks my mother would lash out like a viper. The sting of her mean words was not easily forgotten, even when she was sick and needing render loving care.

———————

My father came to visit me at Nazareth Academy a few rimes. Once he came in the spring and rook me to the Kentucky Derby. Churchill Downs was full of excited people, activity and flowers, yet I was fearful of the repercussions should my father overindulge on the famous Mint Julips. It was the first time in my life that I gambled. I put money on Northern Dancer and he came in first place! My father was impressed with my natural intuition about this horse. It wasn't difficult to see that chis gorgeous high-spirited animal was a winner. I could just feel he would win the race. My intuition was right on target and I was thrilled. Winning that day gave me a sense of self-confidence that had been missing in my life up to char point.

While Dad lived in Costa Rica, he visited several countries in Central America and Mexico. He wrote to me almost every day about his philosophies and points of view on the state of the world. He knew he couldn't be there for me physically, so his letter writing was his best attempt to he supportive of me emotionally. He was consistent with his letters and I looked for them daily because it was the only connection I had with my father. Every Saturday morning at Nazareth, we were taken to the study hall and supervised while we wrote letters to our families and friends. I wrote to my mother, but her responses were infrequent. My favorite letters were to Linda, who was still attending Sr. Mary's Academy in Maryland.

Despite my father's thoughts to the contrary, I graduated from Nazareth Academy, but he did not come to my graduation. He had often said I would end up working in a five-and-dime score and would never amount to anything. Even though he was only char negative and hurtful when he had drunk too much, his criticism hurt my feelings. We children of alcoholics often say to ourselves, "Well, they are on that subject again, so they are good and drunk." My parents had an *anger* issue with each drink they rook and they lashed out at whoever was available, usually me. I know my father was hoping I would join the convene after graduation, but by this time I had realized it didn't matter what I did, he would always find something to criticize about my decision. Nothing I did was ever good enough for him. To this day, I crave approval from the men in my life and have spent a lifetime chasing it. Despite my past, on graduation day the future seemed hopeful. It was the blessing of youth, the contagious joy that came from my other classmates and the fact I finally did accomplish my goal of graduating.

After graduation in 1966, I spent some of the summer in Costa Rica, where my father was working as an engineer. I thought he was working for an American firm, installing a sanitation system near the city of San Jose, but was later told his job had something to do with Naval Intelligence. Since my father had programmed me to *never* ask any questions, I didn't know for sure. So much of what he had done in Europe could have been a cover for his intelligence work there as well. I had grown up instinctively knowing when to ask questions and when not to ask them.

I was grateful to be out of the confines of boarding school and anxious to get on with my life. In Costa Rica I stayed with Sandra, one of my classmates from Nazareth Academy, and her family. Her family was very prominent and I was included in all of their social functions. For the first time in my life, I lived the life of a privileged lady. Sandra and I spent the mornings over coffee looking through fashion magazines to find the right dresses the seamstress could make for us to wear for the following week's *fiesta* and some of the other social functions we were scheduled to attend. Our days were spent looking over fabrics for the intended dresses. Fashion magazines were consulted again when we went to have our ha.ir done for our evening or luncheon engagements. A great deal of time was spent having manicures and pedicures and constant fittings at the seamstress' shop.

This kind of life was totally new to me. My mother didn't use any makeup except lipstick and was allergic to perfume. She was very tailored in her choice of clothing and didn't like most jewelry or scarves around her neck. I was getting in touch with my femininity and enjoying it all, especially since Sandra was there to experience it with me. The family chauffeur even drove us to our different appointments. Soon I was speaking

Spanish again and learning about the culture of Central America. The music, dancing, and food were vibrant. Once again I was in a country pulsing with a passion for living. It felt good to be away from the Midwest with its bland white bread anti spice-less way of life.

While I was there, Dad was living in a hotel, bur he eventually located a two-bedroom apartment. I lived with him for a few weeks before returning to the United States. My father put me in charge of buying what he needed for his apartment: linens, bedding, kitchen items and finding a maid and a cook. I complained to my father after one buying excursion, "I couldn't find any decent linen for the maid and the only pillows they had were stuffed with straw. That's got to be uncomfortable."

"Joni, things are very different here. I don't want to spoil her," he told me.

My father was drinking again and frequently drank himself into a stupor and passed out after our evening meal. I was extremely uncomfortable with his behavior and I decided to leave Costa Rica earlier than planned. I went to spend some time with Leslie and her family at their summer home on Dauphin Island, Alabama. I couldn't wait to escape a situation I couldn't control.

Leslie's family had invited me to stay for a couple of weeks. We spent many days with her younger sister and brothers at the country club pool or on the beach working on our cans. We made peanut butter and jelly sandwiches for all of them and once they were serried at the pool, Leslie, her sister and I spent our time talking the days away while lying on the beach.

It was a memorable time and significant because I observed the relationship between Leslie's parents, Grace and Joe. Regardless of what was going on, Grace and Joe stopped to really communicate with each other. They never seemed to disagree and were ready to really listen to each other. I never heard Grace argue with her husband. It is etched in my memory how she would stop him and gently explain she didn't understand exactly what he meant rather than shout our obscenities and call him an idiot. Here was a family with nine children and Joe and Grace rook rime out every night for their happy hour. They would sit at their kitchen bar and have meaningful conversations while enjoying their martinis. There was no falling down drunkenness and fistfights. Of course, there was the mayhem of nine children and myself all talking, but it made a significant impact on me how a couple could have a chance at happiness together.

4

Endicott College

That fall of 1966 I entered Endicott Junior College, north of Boscon in Beverly, Massachusetts. I was feeling confident about enjoying my classes and excited about meeting my new classmates. Despite my dyslexia, I had high hopes chat I would achieve good grades and succeed.

My first semester I chose an interior design class because I liked beautiful surroundings and it sounded like something I was capable of doing. I found that the women in my class were much more competitive than I had experienced in high school and it made me uncomfortable. Everyone seemed to strive for the highest grade. Trying to be better than ochers spilled over into college fashion. The schools dress code was casual but blue jeans weren't allowed. Female students flaunted their clothing; some wore mink vests or mink coats and there was no shortage of gold and diamonds. They also competed over who would receive the most invitations to the men's Ivy League colleges. Young women were desperately seeking their" MRS" degree, but it had to be with a man who had the proper credentials and pedigree.

Part of our first semester as Endicott freshmen, from before the Thanksgiving holiday until the day after the New Year, was to be spent in an internship in the field of our major. I was instructed to find work with an interior designer somewhere in the United Scares and live there for char duration of time. With no connections anywhere in the US, I was at a loss. Fortunately, Rorie Navin, a classmate, invited me to Morristown, New Jersey, where her parents opened their home and their hearts to me. I couldn't locate a designer immediately, so J found a job as cashier in a downtown Morristown department store. I was promised an eventual position in the furniture section to assist the designer, but I could cell char possibility was highly unlikely. The school wasn't concerned, so J just went with the flow. I was graceful for the hospitality of the Navins', and the job I had turned out to be fun.

Once again I witnessed a happy family, everyone got along very well, and I was impressed with the courtesy they showed each other. Most evenings after supper Mr. and Mrs. Navin, without harsh words or disagreements, would take turns reading poetry to us. As a result of observing both Leslie's parents and Rories parents. I was determined to eventually find a husband who I could talk to and thus discuss whatever was on our minds. I wanted a husband who had the qualities of both Joe Morales and Mr. Navin.

Since my mother was not talented in the kitchen, I had never learned cooking skills. My very first attempt in the kitchen was at Rories house; I helped her mother bake delicious chocolate chip cookies and learned how to make a soft-boiled egg.

For my Christmas gift chat year, my father sent me a first-class airline ticket to meet him in Mexico City for the holidays. When I arrived, which was late at night, I looked for him, but he had forgotten to meet my flight. It wasn't until late morning of the next day that Immigration and the U.S. Embassy found him in a hotel room on a drunken binge.

I wasn't even angry; I did not know how to be angry. Instead, I was angry with myself for not being able to express my disappointment in him to his face. It really hurt and disappointed me to realize I mattered so little that he could forger about my arrival. Confrontation is very difficult for me, almost impossible. I didn't have the cools then to know my feelings had been hurt and I was entitled to an apology. All of my life I had turned my anger inward and swallowed it. I just stuffed it and rook a Valium just like my parents. Much later in life, I realized I have always had a problem getting in couch with my emotions because of the years and years of denying they even existed. I knew nothing about "feelings." I just knew I desperately needed to be loved and something was so wrong about the way I was receiving the little love I was getting.

Despite the holiday's inauspicious beginning, my father cried to entertain me. He rented a car and drove us to Acapulco and then to Taxco, which is a beautiful, silver mining town and typically Mexican. I preferred it to the tourist rat race of Acapulco, where I got too much sun.

My father's drunkenness char Christmas made it one I would never forget. I swore I'd never let a man affect me chat way again on a major holiday, especially my father. He never apologized for forgetting me, but we both acted as if nothing had happened. As I looked out the airplane window on my way back to Massachusetts, I swore chat would be my last Christmas with him.

When I returned to Endicott for my second semester, I tried to contact my good friend, Eva Rivera, from my Nazareth Academy days. I wanted to quit school after my freshman year and move to her hometown in Puerto Rico in the spring so I could be in the emotionally warm Latin American culture I enjoyed so much. I felt accepted there and could easily fie in since I spoke Spanish.

When I called, I was told the devastating news that she had committed suicide. How could she die so young? I couldn't imagine the pain that would cause Eva to take her life. Despite my turbulent upbringing, I had never even thought about making a final exit.

I remembered Eva had a Fervent need for love. Ac graduation she had shown me the diamond bracelet her father had given her. It was a popular gift among people with money, or among people who would like you to think they had money. Eva came from extreme wealth, yet I knew she was unbearably unhappy. Eva had tears in her eyes when she showed me the bracelet, bur I did not dare ask her why because some of us couldn't stand to be known as being unhappy. We were all taught to be poised and to "appear" happy. Somewhere I had learned: "Smile, because you can afford to!" And there you have it-smile, smile, smile!

In my second semester at Endicott, positive things started to happen for me. I met Nancy; we both had rooms in the same dormitory and became close friends. Endicott dorms were converted mansions from a long ago era when servants were an important part of wealthy people's lives. There were several small single rooms in the vast mansions, and we both had one.

She visited me in my room soon after we mer. "Can I look in your closer?" she asked.

"Sure," I said.

"Joni, I'm going to take your skirts and dresses to my room," she said after making an assessment of my clothes. "You definitely need some alterations. Trust me, you will look a lot better in mini skirts."

"I don't know, Nancy... I guess I never really thought about it," I said lamely as I followed her, trusting in her judgment and enjoying the fact that someone cared enough about me to help me. When we got there, she put all the clothes on her bed and got her sewing kit out of her dresser.

"I'm going to cut at least a few inches off all of these," she told me confidently as she took a skirt and proceeded to cut off the bottom. Don t worry, I'll hem them for you too. Don't look so shocked!"

Nancy loved to attend parties, was very jovial and popular and made a point to see that I got invited out as often as she did. Nancy was probably the most beautiful woman I'd ever met and she did not have a vain bone in her body. Because neither of us had chosen a major or had a career planned, I felt better and less lost. Life became fun for me. I discovered alcohol and the effect it had on my feeling shy and awkward. When I drank, it lifted away my anxiety and made me bold. My painful shyness dissipated and I developed a grand state of self-esteem. I didn't realize it at that time, but I began to look forward to drinking alcohol at the parties I attended. The parties became more frequent and so did the drinking.

I had hoped by having a single room I would develop better study habits, but attending college during this time in my life just didn't work for me. I couldn't concentrate on anything and didn't realize these were, for me, early symptoms of manic-depressive illness. I had several sleepless nights in a row, which resulted in my becoming hysterical and ending up sedated with Valium shots in the Endicott infirmary.

I loved the social aspect of college but I was not doing well scholastically. I wrote my father for help in finding an art job somewhere on the East Coast for the following year. He had many contacts all over the country from his days at Penn State, so we agreed I would discontinue my classes the following year at Endicott. I wasn't doing well academically in my other subjects and I wasn't happy in that setting.

I realized later that I just wanted to be out on my own; I was fed up with being supervised.

During the second semester of my freshman year at Endicott. I chose to study fine art, did very well, and finally found a sense of peace in a scholastic setting for the first time since my school days in Spain. Even though I loved fine arts, I had no idea what to do for a career, and I didn't want to remain in school. I had considered becoming a Playboy Bunny because Nancy had suggested it. I even went for the interview—bunny costume and all, but no ears! The lady who dressed me had to pin the costume because I was so tine. She used a half roll of toilet paper stuffed under my breasts to give me cleavage. I almost got the job, but the male interviewer me told me he would be doing me a favor by not hiring me. Think it was just a polite way to tell me I was too skinny and flat-chested. I never told my father or many others about that incident.

During that year, the love and attention I received from my father was erratic; in one moment I felt the warmth of his affection, but in the next moment, he could become cold and cruel. When I was with him, I would close down my feelings to protect myself from his mood swings. When I later attended Adult Children of Alcoholics meetings, I discovered closing down emotionally was a way of coping for *all* children of alcoholics. But ignoring my feelings did not help me to develop into a mature adult, especially when I later tried to build successful relationships of my own.

I had no idea how to be emotionally intimate with anyone. I loved my handsome and domineering father, but our relationship became one of love and hate because of his severe personality disorder, which was most likely manic-depressive illness, not to mention his alcoholism. When I was with him and he was sober, he was very jovial and believed in me one hundred percent, and I felt some affection. Ie was just so difficult to know when he would be "there" for me. At times he would withdraw and disappear for months. I'm sure he was off fighting his own demons and suffering just as badly as I was suffering. Like me, he was prone to bouts of energy and sleepless nights just as he had his depressive moods. In a manic mood one rime, he was able to drive almost nonstop across the country. He quenched his manic behavior with copious amounts of alcohol.

Neither of us knew how to communicate with each other. Through therapy, I later learned that healthy communication skill would have solved many of our problems. While I was young, I was immature and impressionable and rook what my father said and all his actions very personally. I was too self-absorbed and thought what had transpired in our family was my fault. I had to shut down and learn how to detach from my father because of the unbearable emotional pain I was feeling. Once I mastered the art of detachment, I applied it to all my relationships. For me, there had to be a distance from people. I isolated myself from others and consequently suffered from severe loneliness.

The fear of emotional intimacy was just too excruciating to bear until I met Brent Bennett in the spring of his junior year at Harvard, where he was majoring in economics. I was in the dining room of Harvard's Elliot House with my dare, Jay, when Brent and I were introduced. Although I was friendly, I was also reserved and cautious with people. But since I was petite, pretty, and stylish thanks to Nancy, Brent cook an immediate liking to me, got my phone number from Jay and called me. He asked me to come to Harvard for a football game the following weekend.

Since Endicott was about an hour north of Boston, I rook a train and he met me at the station. At first I didn't feel he was preppy enough. Because he came from Columbus, Ohio, I couldn't help but think of the bland, Midwestern flavor I had left behind in Kentucky. However, he was extremely handsome, a couple of inches under six feet with broad, strong shoulders, and had a warm and charming manner chat was difficult to resist. Brent had jet-black hair, a strong jaw and a wide, bright winning smile, just like my father. Until the summer break, I would often cake the train and spend the weekend with him. He was respectful, yet affectionate with me and showed me genuine interest and love, which made me blossom, and I felt safe and protected when I was with him.

Drinking alcohol mixed with cranberry juice was quite popular at most of the college weekends. It had a tart, fruity taste that disguised the alcohol. Drinking waste he main event at all the parties Brent and I attended. We were both moderate to heavy drinkers from the start. It loosened us up and made our relationship smooth and gentle; when we had too much, we'd both fall asleep. Consequently, we took a lot of naps. Drinking didn't alter Brent's outgoing, cheerful personality; he was jovial before, during and after drinking, unlike my parents.

Brent was a wonderful conversationalist and could talk about so many different things. His varied interests included photography, reading Latin, and a desire to travel. He was fascinated and curious about me and wanted to know more about my travels. It wasn't long before I became smitten and discovered sex intermingled with love. I was already twenty and had discovered sex before attending Endicott, but it wasn't enjoyable until I slept with Brent. I had always had a short trial run with men sexually, but I had never gotten past that. With Brent I finally felt the intimate connection. With such a romantic, attentive lover, we ended up spending about ninety percent of our time in bed. He was far more experienced than me, and he guided me through our lovemaking.

That summer Brent returned to Ohio to work for his fathers construction firm, and I went to Washington, D.C. to join my best friend, Linda, my alcove-mate from St. Mary's who worked as a dental hygienist. I had a job at Little Caledonia, a chic gift shop in Georgetown, and we shared a two-bedroom apartment right above a food market on P Street, right in the heart of Georgetown. It was a great place to live because everything we needed was close at hand and we didn't need a care since we could walk everywhere.

Brent came to visit for a long weekend and we both had a marvelous rime. We laughed, played, made love and fell in love as we explored Georgetown and the bars around the university. One night we went to a performance of *Madame Butterfly* at the Watergate floating houseboat on the Potomac. One day we rented a canoe at a place along the Potomac River and had a hilarious time getting our rowing skills to move in sync. Since I ran out of steam as we were crying to return the boat, we paddled madly against the current crying to get the boar back on rime.

My father came to meet Brent and cake us out to dinner. After dinner, he starred to ask Brent some questions about his background. "So, Brent, tell me something about your ancestors."

"Well, Mr. Nebel, I'm a real typical American mix," Brent answered.
"English, German?"

"Not quite, it's a bit more unconventional. I've got some Irish and English ancestors, but we've got some native Indian blood as well. My dad tells me we're related to the Cherokee and the Chippewa," Brent explained.

"Chippewas? They were the dirty ones," my father couldn't resist adding in disgust, not caring what kind of impression he made on Brent. I was embarrassed and tried to change the subject.

Dad called me later and went on and on about Brent's lineage and how he was seriously against my dating him because "things could get serious." I hadn't realized he was so prejudiced. Brent looked exactly like my father did during his college years, so I couldn't imagine that he was serious about this blood thing.

People who knew me well were under the impression that I should have tons of money and could do as I pleased because of my inheritance from my grandmother, but I never shared any details about my finances. I didn't know how to manage to get my money from my father. Dad claimed it was all tied up in stocks. During college, he gave me a monthly allowance and paid my college expenses. I could charge books and art supplies at the campus bookstore, but I didn't ask questions about how things got paid and didn't ask for more than I received in allowance. I didn't know then but discovered later that my father had a gambling problem, especially with his favorites-roulette and craps-and my inheritance trickled through his fingers. I thought he was being stingy with my money and maybe overly cautious, but money never concerned me for long in my young years. As long as I had enough to get by and do what I wanted, I ignored it all.

I was not going back to Endicott in the fall of 1967, so I moved up to Cambridge, Massachusetts to be closer to Brent, ignoring my father's objections to Brent's background. My father located a job for me as a greeting card designer for Rust Craft Greeting Cards in Dedham, Massachusetts. I was excited because it was finally a job chat would be fun for me. I would be doing something I was good at and receiving a paycheck for my time and talent. I was also in love, which made the mood even more magical. I rented a room in a private home of a retired Harvard professor in Cambridge. The professor had taught German and had a wonderful housekeeper who prepared our meals.

Life was very good. I loved my work, and my routine was uncomplicated. I was in a car pool that gathered workers in Cambridge and we drove together to and from Dedham daily. Weekends belonged to Brent would conceal me for the rest of the weekend in the dorm. He lived in a four-bedroom suite with a living room that he shared with three other students. Girls were not permitted in the dorm after a certain time in the evening, but I was quiet and his roommates didn't seem to mind. Brent was in his senior year and interested in keeping up his grades, so I usually brought my paints to keep me busy when he studied. I would paint cute things, like little girl's faces, animals and flowers. That time was like living in never-never land.

When we became engaged in January of 1968, my mother presented me with her solitary diamond engagement ring as a wedding gift. Brent was from a large Catholic family and the oldest of ten children. When we called to cell his parents we were engaged, Brent discovered he had a new baby brother, born the day before.

Brent worked nights as an orderly at the Cambridge City Hospital. He was saving money to buy me a wedding band with six diamonds and arrange a honeymoon in Puerto Rico. Mother Superior and the bishop granted Brent and me permission for our wedding ceremony to be held at the main chapel in Nazareth, Kentucky. We chose Nazareth since I did not have a hometown or a family home at char rime. Our wedding was an important event since there had only been one other marriage performed in this convents church over its very long history.

I felt like Cinderella going to the ball on the morning of the wedding. The nuns made a big fuss over me, scurrying around to help me dress and get all the derails just right. Even though my parents came, the nuns were more like my family. With all the young girls in training to become nuns singing in the choir during the wedding mass, I felt like it was something out of "The Sound Of Music." It was a beautiful and ethereal ceremony, and the choir sounded like angels from heaven.

I was happy but also fearful and somewhat shy about all that was happening to me. Leslie, my first friend from Nazareth, was my maid of honor, and luckily she was calm and jovial. All of my bridesmaids were Nazareth graduates.

My parents brought discord since they argued just as they had when they were married. I was disappointed and frustrated they couldn't see this was a special occasion for all of us. They always seemed to take the opportunity to downplay every special occasion during my life. Their behavior was a turning point for me; from that time on, I was finished caring about what they thought about me or my life.

5

Marriage

It was May 1968 and in the midst of the Vietnam War when we got married. Brent had graduated from Harvard and instead of the risk of being drafted, he wanted to enlist in the U.S. Army and get it over with. He didn't even consider that his bad eyesight would exempt him.

"But, Brent, I don't want you to come home in a coffin," I protested when he began making his plans.

"What makes you think I'll die? Don't you have any faith in me?" Brent retorted.

"War has nothing to do with faith. If you want to join a service, why don't you join the Navy? To my mind, it would be a whole lot safer," I suggested.

"That's not a bad idea, Joni. My father was a Navy fighter pilot. I bet he'd get a kick out of his son as a naval officer."

When Brent entered the Naval Officer Candidate School in Newport, Rhode Island, I was greatly relieved by his decision. Brent had instilled in me a genuine sense of strong self-worth and had encouraged me to come out of my shell, which helped me decide on my career direction. I enjoyed people and loved the idea of becoming a flight attendant. I had applied for and been offered a job with Eastern Airlines. I was overjoyed because everything about the job appealed to me. When

Brent went off to OCS in Newport in early June, I went to Miami to Eastern's training school.

Regardless of how enthused I was about my new job, I knew my father would criticize my choice of profession; he did char no matter what I did. But I was starring to move forward and finally making my own decisions without concerning myself about my father's feeling and judgements. I distanced myself from my father as far as I could. His criticism had been wearing me down.

After only six weeks of training, my first base with Eastern Airlines was in Boston. Being in love and newly married, we tried to see each other as often as possible. Brent had weekend leave while at OCS, and drove to Boston from Newport for a romantic two days every weekend.

I was concerned about our new marriage and made one important request of Brent before he graduated from OCS: char he try to get shore duty. I explained to him I wanted and needed for us to be together so we could learn how to make our marriage work. Because of my upbringing, I had no earthly idea what a good marriage could possibly entail, and I did not know what a wife was supposed to do. The closest I had ever come to running a home was during the shore summer weeks I spent in Costa Rica in my father's apartment. I was in charge of celling the cook what to prepare for the meals. The maid seemed to know what to do when she cleaned, so I didn't even learn how to clean a home firsthand. I hadn't even cooked a meal! Using a cookbook received as a wedding gift, my first cooking efforts were almost disastrous. I accidentally switched the salt and sugar, putting a cup of salt in the cheesecake and a cup of sugar in the spaghetti. I had a great deal to learn about how to keep up a home and how to be a wife!

Brent graduated ninth in his class at OCS and could have had any tour of duty he wanted. He chose to go to sea when I desperately needed him by my side. T needed him more than he needed me, so I cook chis issue very personally and resented Brent for his decision. This was the weakest point in our marriage and probably the turning point. I was angry with him, yet my fear of confrontation caused me to back down. Brent and I didn't know how to communicate with each other out of bed. Eventually my anger caused me to be unfaithful to him.

After Brent's graduation, he was sent to Brunswick, Georgia, for Combat Information Center training for his future position aboard a destroyer. I cook a month's leave of absence from my airline job and lived in Brunswick with Brent while he attended the training school. It was my first effort to play house and I thoroughly enjoyed it. I busied myself with grocery shopping, cooking and making things like curtains. I had gotten skillful enough in the culinary arts to make pies and bake my own bread. I was attempting to make our little beach cottage into a home.

Brent's first tour of duty was in Newport as a combat information officer aboard his new ship. We lived in Navy housing for about two months before the ship sailed for Norfolk, Virginia. Since the ship was going to be in Norfolk for about six weeks, I transferred my airline base from Boston to Washington, D.C. Norfolk wasn't that far from the District of Columbia, and we spent time in both places.

When his ship left for the Mediterranean to be with the Seventh Fleet, I moved into the house I inherited from my grandmother. My mother had moved in while I was in training school in Miami. She had come to nurse my grandfather, who had been ill with cancer of the throat. He died on July 4th, as my grandmother had nine years earlier, and I got leave from my training to attend the funeral in Washington. Mother went off the deep end with my grandfather's death and was drinking around the clock after I moved in. I asked Roger, who was still living there, not to by her alcohol, but she pleaded with him. Not able to resist her pleas, he gave in and life then became intolerable for me.

I realized about two months after Brent's ship left that I was pregnant. Because I was being harassed by my mother whenever I was home. I didn't give my health the attention it deserved. She chased me around the house, calling me names at all hours of the night, continually yelling at me about my being a bitch and not deserving to be married to a man who had attended Harvard. I didn't want to tell her I was pregnant because she was so hateful, resentful and mean when she drank. I wasn't sure what she would have done with the information. Eventually I had to call Alcoholics Anonymous to get some help with her. She was so drunk most of the time that she was continually hurting herself falling down the stairs or tripping and bumping into things. It became and endless struggle for me to put up with her as she went in and out of hospital psychiatric wards.

I had a pretty difficult schedule being based in Washington, D.C., and commuting to Baltimore almost daily. It was a rugged routine with odd hours since I flew mostly night coaches back and forth to Puerto Rico, because of my ability to speak Spanish. I was not getting enough rest, and absolutely no relaxation at home with my mother, and therefore lost my baby. After the miscarriage I went to my gynecologist, who recommended I take some time off, get out of my chaotic living situation, and visit with my husband while he was stationed in the Mediterranean Sea. The Doctor told me I was burning the candle at both ends, which was endangering my health.

With a letter from my doctor, Eastern Airlines granted me a leave of absence to follow Brents ship around the Mediterranean. I didn't tell him I had been pregnant or about my mother's problems, since he already disapproved of her falling-down drunkenness. I just told him I wanted to be near him and do some traveling. I was afraid that he would insist I quit my job with the airlines if he knew the truth. It was a very exciting time to be in Europe with Brent. We didn't have very much money, but in those days it really was possible to live on five dollars a day in Europe. We were young, didn't need anything lavish, and preferred what was affordable for us.

For Christmas 1969, Brent surprised me when he accounted, while the ship was anchored in Cannes, that he had a two-week leave. I was thrilled because we hadn't had much time alone together since the ship left Norfolk. With my airline discounts, I was able to buy us both round-trip tickets on Swiss Air to Geneva, Switzerland. Upon arriving, we were surprised when Swiss immigration authorities requested we go immediately to our hotel and stay there until they checked to see if Brent was "genuinely" on leave from the U.S. Navy. They were afraid Brent would be seeking asylum in Switzerland due to the Vietnam situation.

Once everything was in order, we explored and loved Genova, where we had genuine Swiss fondue and wandered around the lovely old section of the city. We took the train to Zermatt, which was at the foot of the Matterhorn in the Swiss Alps. We had no idea that the very elite went there for their winter holidays. We just thought it would be a nice place to spend the Christmas holidays and we were right! It was like a fairy tale, and Brent seemed to enjoy the new sights and sounds as much as I did.

Our hotel room was tiny but decorated in the very best of Swiss tradition— complete with goose-down quilt! To top it off, our window overlooked a babbling brook and the local church graveyard. On Christmas

Eve, every grave was lit with a candle. With the deep snow and all the candles, the effect was magical. The only mode of transportation in Zermatt back then was by horse drawn sleigh. The sounds of sleigh bells jingling on the horses, the swishing of the sleighs in the snow and the smell of wood burning in the fireplaces throughout the village, created a magical Christmas spirit. Even though we only ate twice a day to keep to our budget, we ate well and the food was exceptionally good.

During those months in the Mediterranean, I was able to see several different countries, including Malta and other remote places. I also traveled by both train and plane throughout Europe, discovering I had a passion to travel. I loved learning about foreign countries and the people in these faraway places. I was fortunate I was an airline employee; I received a sizable discount wherever I went, not only on the airlines, but in hotels as well.

I didn't realize it at the time, but during those early years of traveling, I experienced the first signs of my manic-depressive illness that would begin to manifest more obviously as I grew older. The lack of structure in my lifestyle at that time helped to mask the symptoms of my severe emotional sensitivity. As long as I was flitting from place to place, I never had the time to face myself or to discover what I really wanted out of life. Traveling was a way to avoid facing my illness.

After his tour of duty in the Mediterranean, Brent was assigned to be the Aide to the Commandant of the Naval District in Washington, D.C. We were given housing in the Washington Navy Yard. This might have been a perfect time for me to quit my job with the airlines and start a family, but I did not want to give up my career and was even toying with the idea of getting into airline management. Brent and I had briefly discussed having a family, but he didn't express any real enthusiasm. We both had our minds on career pursuits and the idea of a family soon became a forgotten subject.

Brent's job provided us with housing, but he never offered my any money. I didn't know how to approach him on the subject, so I thought my financial needs were my responsibility. I was too afraid to give up my job with the airline and lose my financial security. I decided to remain a flight attendant and not go into management because my working hours would have prevented me from spending much time with Brent and I wouldn't have been able to travel very much.

In the back of my mind, one of the primary reasons I didn't give serious thought to having a baby was my mother. For me, motherhood represented a lifetime commitment of **total** unselfishness and being tied down to a serious responsibility. The idea of being so responsible for another human being scared me. I just could *not* make that kind of commitment. I had my mother to contend with, as well as my career and my marriage, and it seemed to me that the role of mother would be a career in itself. It was a terrible time for me. I knew that motherhood could be a good experience, but with my difficult childhood memories, I knew it could be hell as well, especially for my child. I became concerned about population growth in general and joined both Zero Population Growth and Planned Parenthood. I even had my cat fixed!

After Roger died, I inherited my grandmothers house and Brent and I began renovating it for resale. My mother, still a falling-down drunk, had been living there alone. Since she had nowhere else to go, she came to live with us in Navy housing, which was far from the ideal solution. Brent did not like my mother and didn't hide his feelings; at times they squabbled like children. He never forgot how she had carelessly given away a cherished and lovely crystal decanter, a wedding gift from a friend of Brent's. She never revealed the reason for her action and refused to tell us to whom she had given it.

I needed to get my mother away from Brent for awhile, so I took her to Hong Kong and Hawaii soon after she moved in. Mother loved the Orient, and we both had a comfortable time with each other. We enjoyed our many tours and shopping for souvenirs. In Hong Kong, Mother had some clothes made-to-order from a Chinese tailor in Kowloon.

We had a hilarious time trying to order mushroom soup in a Hong Kong restaurant. My mother had a craving for this particular soup and we found a tiny restaurant we thought would be ideal and attempted to explain what we wanted. I spoke no Chinese and the staff spoke no English. With sign language, we managed to get a soup bowl, but it was filled with hot water with a sole mushroom floating in the middle—so much for our wishful thinking and our knowledge of Chinese cuisine. It sure wasn't Campbell's!

Mother cried when we got off the plane in Honolulu. "You know, Joni, I never believed I would ever see the 'territory where you were born again. I was happier in Hawaii than any other place I ever lived."

"I'm so glad we could do this trip together, Mother. I also feel a real connection to Hawaii," I replied.

"Your Hawaiian godmother told me about an old Hawaiian custom, Joni. When you leave the island by ship, you have to throw your flower lei into the ocean. If the flowers reach the shore, you will return to Hawaii. I threw both our leis in the water just as I was told. They must have reached the shore because my dream came true."

On our trip together I saw a side of my mother that was terribly vulnerable, naive and fragile. She was probably too fragile. My mother and I drank on this trip, but only moderately until one night on Maui. We had bought a bottle of vodka when the plane stopped in Guam for refueling and decided to share the vodka in our Maui hotel. For once we were on the same level getting high together. We laughed, jumped on the bed and jokingly pushed each other. At that time I finally realized my mother was no threat to me. We were more like sisters. I felt closer to her than I had ever felt before. It was true friendship. I kept an eye on her and she obeyed my wishes and did her best not to embarrass me by drinking too much for the duration of our vacation.

When I woke up the next morning with a distressing hangover, my mother gave me a Valium. I was surprised by her offer and especially when she told me Valium was the solution for a hangover and the shakes.

In Maui we rented a car and took off to explore the northern part of the island. We had been told about the little town of Hana and the Seven Sacred Pools. Hana at the time was like never-never land. Looking for a spot to have a picnic, we stumbled onto the most beautiful series of waterfalls that cascaded from the land down into the sea. The vegetation was green, lush and vibrant; it was like being in a fantasy world. We were both so utterly and absolutely amazed at such beauty that it left us speechless.

We wandered out onto the cliffs to continue looking at all this magical beauty, not aware of the threatening gray clouds forming above us. Suddenly, the sky opened up and we were drenched! We squealed like pigs and ran breathlessly through the pouring rain to the car. Inside the car, we looked at each other and cracked up laughing. We were a pitiful and soggy sight! That day was the happiest memory I have of being with my mother. When I look back, I feel that is the way mothers and daughters would always like to feel.

Back in Washington, my mother reverted to her old drinking habits. With her petite physique, it didn't take much alcohol for her to get drunk and then her personality would change and it would be difficult to control her. She was living with us in the Washington Navy Yard, but since I was commuting out of Washington and flying out of Newark, New Jersey, I wasn't home as much and Brent had to deal with her. Drunk, loud and aggressive, she had made a spectacle of herself at the Officers' Club and the store in the Navy Yard, Her behavior was embarrassing Brent and putting his job in jeopardy. One night she got very drunk in front of both of us. When Brent tried to restrain her, she bit him on the hand and drew blood. She was literally like a wild animal, and we had to put her in a hospitals psychiatric ward that night. Luckily, my father still had her on his insurance policy, despite the fact he had remarried, and she was provided with the best medical care possible at that time.

Brent and I attended the weekly family group therapy sessions at the hospital with my mother. All the other patients had their spouses or parents there. I was the only one with a parent as a patient. Because I was overwhelmed with the situation, I kept my mouth shut and let Brent deal with it. During these sessions I learned about role-reversal: Brent and I were playing the parental role, and I didn't like the role I was forced to take on bit. It caused me to decide for certain not to have any children of my own. I had no specific expectations of Brent; I felt he was doing his best and I was praying for a miracle to solve our difficulties. But the other patients and their families criticized Brent for his lack of compassion, and we were both accused of being heartless and too remote. I didn't think they had the right to criticize him, after all she was his mother-in-law, not his mother.

I didn't know what to feel; it was a living nightmare and I was extremely confused. My mother's psychiatrist told me I had to choose between my mother and Brent. The psychiatrist wanted me to remain behind in Washington and support my mother and ignore my obligation as a wife to Brent. Once again, I felt my emotions challenged by a situation beyond my control. In weighing my decision I remembered that my mother *had* disappointed me in the past, and I didn't think she'd ever change. My husband had only disappointed me when he chose sea duty over shore duty in 1969. I chose to stay with my husband since I loved him and felt my place was beside him, but my decision left me with the terrible feeling I had abandoned my mother and left her feeling devastated. Thirty years later I still feel the guilt. Now I can see I was too immature to make such a responsible decision, but I don't think my mother ever forgave me for abandoning her.

Back in 1972 I was too blind to see just how selfish, overbearing and self centered Brent and I were. Fortunately, after living in a halfway house for a while, my mother moved into her own Washington apartment and found a job as a registered nurse in a small hospital nearby. She did not know how to drive but enjoyed walking to and from work. Brent had completed his military obligation and we were planning to leave Washington for Massachusetts where he would be taking pre-med courses at Harvard. Since Mother seemed to be settled, I thought it was safe to leave her on her own. Besides, I had been raised to believe that my husband was the one to be obeyed.

After selling my grandmothers house, we applied some of the money to the home we were building in Hamilton, Massachusetts, which was in the country. The new house was a three-bedroom, two-story house on five acres of property that was zoned for horses. It was a dream come true for two young people. On a whim, typical of my behavior in those years, I had chosen Hamilton as a home base, even though we had no family or friends there.

6

Exploring Together

Brent and I went to Rome for New Year's to visit my father and his new bride, Ysabel. For about a year they had been living in Ravenna, Italy, studying under a private mosaic master and they took the train down to meet us. Mosaic technique was a consuming interest for both of them; before coming to Italy they had lived and studied in San Miguel de Allende, a funky artists' colony in Mexico, and both had received a master's degree in mosaic techniques.

Ysabel was one of the most delightful women I'd ever met. At sixty-two, the same age as my father, she was beautiful, elegant and talented, and had a jolly disposition. She was petite, with lovely white hair, bright blue eyes and rosy cheeks. I desperately wanted Ysabel to like me. She could feel my fondness for her and returned the feeling, but it was obvious to her that I was very needy and wanted some kind of normal mother figure. She cautioned me not to try to replace my mother with her.

My father, who always had a good sense of humor when he was sober, had always told me it was very important to laugh. He was true to his word by marrying a lady who not only found my father amusing, but made him laugh as well.

Ysabel had a daughter and son living in San Francisco. On a later trip, we met Ysaber's children, my new stepsister and stepbrother, their spouses and their children. I was amazed that I suddenly had a delightful and accepting family, something good and positive I had never dreamed of having. I couldn't believe my good fortune! They were all attractive, kindhearted, bright, and had fun-loving personalities, and I immediately adopted them with all my heart.

After we sold my grandmother's house and built our house in Hamilton in the spring of 1972, we had enough money left over for a trip to Europe and a new car. We could afford both because our flights were free thanks to my job. Brent had been discharged from the Navy and I was granted a three-month leave of absence from the airlines. We ordered a Volvo station wagon, which we picked up in Sweden, and then drove the car from Sweden to Europe via Finland and Russia. We took a ferry from Stockholm, Sweden, to a coastal town in Finland.

Both of us liked to drink, but neither of us had witnessed anything like the drinking we saw on that ferry. Since sleeping compartments were hard to come by, we had to stay in the public lounges where we could see that almost everyone on the entire ship was so drunk by 4:00 a.m. they had passed out everywhere. We sat and gazed at the midnight sun; we couldn't have walked anywhere because of the inebriated bodies lying all over the deck. I was angry and bothered by it since it reminded me of my parents' behavior. I had thought my trip would take me far away from such memories.

When we arrived in Helsinki, we went to check in with the Russian Intourist travel agency office and discovered there had been a major mistake. The tourist lodges were not open until July, but at least the campsites were available for camping. Not wanting to pass up the opportunity to see Russia, we decided we would camp. We put off buying camping equipment because we wanted to see what was available in Leningrad. When we arrived at the camp outside Leningrad, we located someone who spoke a little English. All we could rent were some old smelly air mattresses and scratchy blankets we were sure were left over from the last war.

The next day we investigated the G.U.M. department store in Leningrad, known in 1972 to be the largest department store in the world. But there was very little merchandise for sale. Many of the things on display were just that, only for show. Finally, we found two quilts we were sure were stuffed with horsehair. These quilts and our car were our sleeping accommodations for the next few weeks.

Since we couldn't speak Russian, we had a tough time locating food. At the campsite, we managed to figure out how to order eggs baked in a metal dish. I found a marker in downtown Leningrad and stood in a long line outside the shop for what seemed like forever. I had to tell them in Russian what I wanted and pay for it before it could be purchased, which was a torturous process. I was given a funnel of newspaper to fill with what I wanted. The selection was grim and included withered cabbage, moldy potatoes and limp carrots. I bought cans of meat, but it was so mushy I had no idea what we ate. When one is hungry many things prove to be edible! The beer was absolutely the worst in the world, but we didn't dare drink the water.

The only eventual advantage we had in purchasing what we needed was the Dollar Store, which was recommended by a female Intourist guide when we visited Moscow. The Dollar Store had been established for foreigners and only accepted foreign currency—no rubles allowed. We were able to buy champagne for a future celebration, and gourmet items like caviar. We hadn't known that tourists weren't supposed to shop with ordinary Russians, thus ending up seeing more of the USSR than they would have preferred. It was enough to know that our great enemy was not as modern or strong as they would have wanted Americans to believe.

Everywhere we went, the young people begged us to sell them our precious blue jeans. We had brought few clothes and weren't willing to pan with our jeans. They also wanted to exchange the books they'd read for fresh American books and also asked if we had a postcard from the United States. I think any postcard from the free world would have sufficed. I had brought the historical book, *Nicholas and Alexandra,* with me and when I finished reading it, I traded with a student for an American western.

After having such a wonderful time seeing the Kirov ballet perform in Leningrad, in Moscow we had our first hot shower and then attended the Bolshoi ballet performance, which was also superb! Getting back to the campsite afterward was tricky. The rulebook we had been given was ridiculous for Westerners; it stated that driving was not allowed after dark and using headlights was Forbidden! Somehow we managed to negotiate a potholed road for about ten miles without our headlights, but we never understood that bizarre rule.

Brent and I went to Russia mainly to find out what communism was all about. After seeing the country and its people, I knew in my heart that it was only a matter of time before those curious, drab and truly unhappy Russians changed their government. I'm glad we took our trip while we were young and able to endure the physical discomforts and the authoritarian Soviet attitude.

Hungary was a breath of fresh air. We stayed in a private home with an elderly widow and ate well for the first time in several weeks. We were surprised she did not have hot running water, and had to boil gallons of hot water for our bath. We left sludge in the tub when we were finished. The hot shower in Moscow had been weeks ago. After all we had endured in Russia, I treasured the memory of that deep, luxurious hot bath. Our hostess, who was friendly, generous and good-natured, was genuinely interested in our wellbeing; she hated both the communist government and the Russians.

Vienna was heaven with its abundance of coffeehouses with the most delicious cakes and different flavored coffees. I hadn't been much of an advocate of Coca-Cola before our camping trip, but suddenly I had a serious change of heart for anything American or anything representing the free world!

Our major problem during the trip was a lack of money. We had mistakenly based our budget on the price of gas in the United States, which was far cheaper than in Europe. Since we had almost run out of spending money, we had to cut our trip short and return to our new home in Hamilton. The house was still unfinished; it had no screens and the mosquitoes reminded us of our Russian ordeal.

We only stayed a year in that house because of its distant location from where we needed to be. It was a long commute to Boston's Logan airport for me, and Brent, who re-entered Harvard to continue pre-med courses, had to commute to Cambridge on the train. Our work and school schedules and long commutes began to come between us. Besides, we didn't have much luck making friends in the Hamilton area.

In the spring of 1973, after school was out, we rented our Hamilton house and moved into the Harvard married students' quarters. During the summer, taking advantage of my free flights, we took a trip to the Orient and a few months later went to Buenos Aires and Rio de Janeiro to celebrate Brent's birthday. That fall, as Brent became absorbed in attending classes during the day and working as an orderly at Cambridge City Hospital at night, he began acting distant and totally dissatisfied with me. He complained we were spending too much money on travel and that this money should be going to his medical education. I didn't know at the time that his attentions were being diverted by all the cute nurses and female medical students he was seeing almost daily.

I worked the Boston Shuttle for months, hoping that my being home every night would improve things between us, but it didn't help one bit. In spite of his complaints, in the spring of 1974 I invited Brent to join me on a six-week safari starting in Nairobi. He was totally disinterested so I went alone, knowing that I probably wouldn't have a chance at a trip like this again. The trip allowed me to forget about increasingly intense marital difficulties. Since the cost was reasonable, I even added South Africa to my itinerary. I borrowed a movie camera from a friend and made my own documentary of my African trip. I met interesting people everywhere I went—doctors, photographers, journalists, accountants, diplomats, teachers, etc. It was the best thing I could have done for myself because my world felt broader and more exciting. I discovered travel was my greatest passion and that I enjoyed traveling alone.

While staying at the guest lodge at the Ngorongoro Crater in Tanzania, I met a fellow tourist, an accountant from New Zealand. Since we enjoyed each others company, we reconnected after the safari to spend about a week together in Nairobi, meeting expatriates and sampling colonial English activities such as cricket and archery tournaments. After I took my South African side trip, I joined my new friend in London and he showed me the famous city sights for two weeks.

When I got home, Brent announced he wanted a divorce. He told me I needed a more extensive education to be a doctors wife, and both of us couldn't afford to attend school at the same time. Brent was growing increasingly arrogant, and I probably didn't realize it because of my own father's superior attitude. Ray, a friend of my father's, enlightened me when he told me he had originally wanted to offer Brent financial assistance for his medical schooling, but decided against it. Ray had gotten to know

Brent, when he stayed with him in San Francisco during one of my husband's trips to do interviews with potential medical schools. "Brent already knows it all, Joni," Ray told me. "He was so arrogant about his talents that I didn't feel I could approach him and offer him help."

One of my greatest regrets at that time was an opportunity I had to pass up that may have saved my marriage. The Washington Medical Center offered to train me free-of-charge as a licensed practical nurse, if I served as a volunteer for the Tom Dooley Foundation. They wanted flight attendants to teach hygiene to the poor natives in Southeast Asia, where they had converted houseboats into floating medical clinics, and high up in the mountains of Nepal. Pan Am offered flight attendants free airfare to Nepal if they were chosen to do volunteer medical work. But there was a Catch-22. Eastern Airlines wouldn't give me the leave of absence for the six months of training and Pan. Am wouldn't give me the free airfare if I was not a flight attendant. Brent initially showed great interest in this project and said he would go if I would go, but we had other obstacles to consider, like the time required and our finances. I was the main breadwinner and the logistics of the situation was too difficult to work out. If I could have gone, I might have proved to him that my efforts were worthwhile and that I was trying to improve my life, my career and our marriage. I was discouraged that the airlines wouldn't cooperate with me and give me my leave of absence, but I was too scared to quit my job because it was the only real security I had ever known.

Eventually Brent and I agreed on a legal separation. I insisted on that kind of separation because I felt Brent would outgrow his restless state. He had become too full of himself, and I felt the need to be away from him. I hoped Brent would stay single long enough to outgrow his arrogance and we would be reunited someday. I still loved him and felt we had deep ties between us, so much so that our love would never die.

In the meantime I moved to Atlanta, Georgia, a difficult place for me to live since I didn't have a network of supportive friends there. I was lonely when I wasn't working, but I didn't stay that way for long. I met Alan, a captain who flew for Eastern, and we hit it off. We adjusted our monthly schedules to use my Atlanta apartment during our two weeks of required flying, and then spent the other two weeks at his trendy apartment in Marina Del Rey, near the ocean in Los Angeles. He had a sailboat and we enjoyed ourselves, drinking, sailing or just goofing around.

The affair didn't last. One day when we were out sailing, I noticed several sharks around the boat. Alan was drunk and angry about something and threatened to throw me overboard. I took him seriously, and that night when we were back in his apartment and he was asleep, I left him. He was Jewish and had a cup decorated with what looked like Hebrew writing, but when it was turned upside-down, it said "Fuck You." Before I left that night, I put my house key under that cup on his kitchen counter. My message to him was quite clear!

Back in Atlanta, I asked Brent to come for a visit and he accepted. Alan was also in Atlanta that weekend and wanted me to reconsider ending our affair. He invited me to his hotel to talk and I took Brent with me. Nothing was settled during our meeting, but afterward Brent told me, "I think Alan's an ass. You can do far better than him." I followed Brent's advice.

Brent continued to use my airline passes to fly down for visits. We still felt connected at a soul level, so there seemed to be an air of unfinished business about our relationship, but not enough to keep it going.

7

Around the World

Shortly after my breakup with Alan, I decided I needed a good long break and took advantage of a 90% discount on a Pan Am around-the-world trip. I bought a single ticket and boarded a flight to Rome, which then continued on to Istanbul.

Before we landed in Istanbul, a gentleman from the U.S. Embassy advised me to be extremely careful not to go anywhere in the city alone since twelve white American women had disappeared since January and could have been forced into white slavery. He told me Turkey was a terribly dangerous country in which to be alone and female.

After I got settled into my hotel, I made reservations to take an American Express night tour, which consisted of seeing Istanbul after dark, dinner in a restaurant overlooking the Bosphorus, and an evening of entertainment at a nightclub. It was my first opportunity to observe genuine belly dancers in action. There was one drawback to the evening— the tour guide later tried to get into my room. He was both sneaky and terribly sleazy, so it was a real insult!

The next day I took a tour of the city, which included a visit to the bazaar. Nothing was a bargain and everything looked cheap, gaudy, and unnecessary. The last thing I needed was extra stuff to haul around the world with me!

That night I departed for Beirut, Lebanon, and on the flight I met a professor from the University of California, Berkeley. He was a very interesting man who was going to Beirut on behalf of the US Government to speak about and work with Middle Eastern governments on the displaced Palestinian situation. He mentioned his hotel was only ten dollars a night and offered to make arrangements through the US Embassy for me to receive the same price on my room. That night in Beirut I was grateful to have a reasonably priced bed to sleep in, since I was still at the beginning of my trip and needed to conserve my money.

My first impression of Beirut revealed a clean, peaceful and pretty city filled with Arabic architecture and the flavor of the Middle East. I discovered the real truth when my professor friend and I walked to the US Embassy to pick up a free copy of *Newsweek* magazine. I was shocked when we turned a corner to find a tank aimed at us, flanked by men with machine guns. The embassy building was surrounded with sandbags and barbed wire and we decided not to go through the rigmarole of security checks and red tape. My first introduction to the volatile situation in the Middle East was frightening, yet I was fortunate to have seen Beirut before it lost much of its old charm and beauty.

A fellow flight attendant had given me several stacks of photographs to deliver to his family in Beirut. I called this family and they picked me up for a visit with them. Never in my life have I been greeted so openly and lovingly. These wonderful Lebanese people treated me as if I were a member of their family and took me all over their country. They fed me delicious and mysterious Middle Eastern foods and took me into the mountains to pick figs.

We traveled toward the Syrian border, and when I got out to look around, I spotted a car whose back seat was filled with women covered in the traditional black veils with little peepholes to look through. Since they were giggling and pointing straight at me, I knew they were women. I imagine that my jeans and skinny body must have appeared equally weird to them. My hosts took me to visit other relatives, and when we arrived after a long drive, we were greeted, seated in the shade, and offered bowls of the most delicious, succulent pears, apples and grapes I've ever eaten! When we attended a wedding in a local village, I was startled by the firecrackers and the passion of the people, but liked the atmosphere and the people's ability to express their excitement. These lovely Lebanese people took me to the airport, wished me well, smothered me with hugs and kisses, and gave me a box of baklava that easily could have fed a small tribe of hungry people!

My next stop was Iran, but I was not spending time there, and something made me freeze in my seat. When I looked out the window, I could sense a dark and uninviting atmosphere, which had an evil aura about it. The sensation was so ominous, I did not get off for the short time we were there. When we left, the plane was full of noisy children and lively people dressed in their colorful native dress. The aroma from the exotic foods they brought on board permeated the plane. I remember thinking I wouldn't be able to sleep with all the noise, but I did.

At dawn, the bulging 747 landed in New Delhi, India, and disgorged a huge number of people into the immigration and customs area. Four or five men were doing the work of one person. All my life I had heard how overly populated India was. Finally I could see evidence of this problem. My father had asked me to try to skip India, since he thought the poverty would be too unbearable for me to witness. He made me promise that I would absolutely avoid Calcutta and Bombay because he knew I had a soft spot in my heart for the poor. I had expected to arrive in a country where people would be begging on the runway and in the airport, but this was not the case. I saw what my father meant when I visited downtown New Delhi. There were homeless people in rags and plenty of flies everywhere. Begging women would pinch their children, whose pitiful cries would then attract more money from the tourists.

I had hoped to get on an immediate flight to Nepal, but since I had just missed the plane, I could not get out for two days because there was no daily service to Katmandu. I asked the ticket agent if he could suggest a place for me to stay in the interim, and he told me to wait until he got off duty and he would take me to an inn. Not long after we took off down the street on his motorbike with me on the rear hanging on for dear life. Fortunately, I wasn't overloaded with baggage, but I still had to balance my suitcase, garment bag, and purse while holding onto him. When we encountered a herd of white water buffalo, he simply zigzagged right through them! Despite my precarious position, I noticed everything. Women who weren't poor walked gracefully along the road in silk and cotton saris in the most vibrant colors—oranges, blues and brilliant pinks. India was all so new, so colorful and exciting to me!

The owner of the inn, in a white sari and veil, greeted us at the door. A huge, one-story home with a kitchen and dining room in one area and several bedrooms close-by, the inn was a curious place. I smiled at a small man who was squatting on the floor stirring a curry. When he smiled back I noticed he was toothless and cross-eyed. My senses were alive on this very hot, humid day. The smell of curry, helped along by the ceiling fan, permeated the air; in the background I could hear a television and the whining sound of Indian music. On the way to my room, I noticed a room with an altar, which was cluttered with candles, incense, pictures and plastic flowers.

I would sleep in a room that seemed like a dormitory because there were so many beds. In the bathrooms, there were no shower curtains or hot water. I was accustomed to Western ideas of comfort, like hot running water and rugs, things that were useless in the tropics. There were only white sheets on the beds, no bedspreads. After looking around a little, I could appreciate that the inn was totally adapted to the tropical environment.

Although it was still early in the day, I was tired, so I went to bed. It was dark when I woke up, and I could see many hot and exhausted-looking people quietly coming into the room and getting into bed. They were Australians from a charter flight, who were on their way home from England. I went back to sleep since I planned a little sightseeing for the next day.

I had always wanted to see the Taj Mahal, so I took a tour bus to nearby Agra the next morning. Although the bus was advertised as being "airconditioned," I discovered that meant the windows were open! It was worth it because the building, which is in the middle of nowhere, was quite an impressive and magical sight. The exquisite white Taj Mahal stood majestically amidst the dry red earth; I would never forget its brilliant beauty.

The following day I managed to get on the flight to Katmandu, the capital city of Nepal. Most of the people arriving at the airport were either serious trekkers or on business. This city, which at that time was still fairly small and not as popular a tourist attraction as it would later become, was more of a culture shock to me than India. At that time the streets of Katmandu were dirt and the sewers were open, yet it was breathtaking to be in that valley surrounded by the magnificent Himalayas. To me, Katmandu was the epitome of a meeting place where East meets West.

I found a little bar/restaurant where I went for a Coke and some lunch. "Hello, could I please sit down and converse with you?" a nice looking man with a heavy accent asked me soon after I sat down.

"Sure. Be my guest," I said in my polite airline voice.

"My name is Boris," the man said with a charming smile. His thick head of dark hair framed intelligent brown eyes. I could tell he was at ease with women and I hoped he would provide me with some stimulating conversation.

"Hello, Boris, I'm sure you can tell I'm an American," I laughed. "Tell me about yourself." I was used to letting men control the conversation.

"I am Russian born but as a scientist, I have my own independent ideas. The Russians decided I was too much trouble to keep and they let me emigrate to Israel. A happy turn of events, I must say. But what about you?"

"My name is Joni and I work for the airlines. It's a marvelous way to travel the world for very little money." I paused deliberately, I didn't want to get into my personal life and ruin my fun.

"My friend Israel and I," Boris continued, "we saved our money as well. We came by train from the south of India. We got off the train in New Delhi and we have walked here. The walking was perhaps easier than being on a crowded train full of pungent odors." We both laughed at his revelation.

I was right about Boris' power of conversation; we talked so long it was time for dinner. Israel joined us and suggested we get together with some other acquaintances for a meal. We were an assortment of many nationalities and many accents, but everyone was speaking English, so I didn't miss out on anyone's tale of adventure.

Boris and I became lovers. I was attracted to his brilliance as well as his strong and demanding sexuality. We spent several nights on the hotel roof drinking beer and soaking up the magnificence of Katmandu's exotic mountain setting.

We took a tour together of the three towns and the temples that surround Katmandu. To an American eye, the sexually provocative carvings on the temples were quite scandalous. Cows freely wandering the streets intrigued me and I learned why the Hindus honor cows and believe them to be sacred. Long ago and at a time when the poor were starving and the rich were eating all the beef, a holy man told the people it was wrong to eat meat but holy to drink milk. The cow became a holy animal, and the poor got some nourishment. Coming out of buildings in

Katmandu, I would frequently find that I had to crawl over a cow. They were rather large and seemed fond of doorways!

On the day I was to leave Nepal for New Delhi, there was mass confusion at the airport. Sikkim, a nearby Indian state, had been invaded by the Chinese, and almost everyone wanted to get out of Nepal. At the airport I spotted a tall man with white hair, who I recognized as Dr. Verne Chaney, the doctor who had been instrumental in establishing the Tom Dooley Foundation. Since I had once wanted to be a volunteer with them, I introduced myself and told him my predicament—that I was flying stand-by and had no chance of getting a flight out that day. He took my ticket and passport and somehow got me on the flight with him bound for New Delhi.

We stayed at the same hotel and that night he invited me to join him for supper in the hotel dining room. I hadn't been in a genuine hotel (in the Western sense) since Istanbul. It was nice for a change to have Western comforts. Dr. Chaney was a charming and interesting dinner companion and shared some of his history. Dr. Tom Dooley, who had died at a young age from cancer, had been his best friend. But before he died, Dr. Chaney promised Tom he would carry on with his work in Southeast Asia and Nepal. Dr. Chaney orchestrated the organization so that medical personnel could take free health care into the remote areas that had no medial service for the poor. That evening we exchanged phone numbers. He would be returning to the US, and I was going on to Singapore.

While touring Singapore, I met a young Australian woman to pal around with. It was great to have a woman to talk to and eat with. I had expected a City like Hong Kong, but there was no similarity at all. Singapore, which had a wonderful atmosphere, was very modern and quite clean and seemed to be more Western in nature, despite its location. We went to Raffles, the famous British built hotel with its uniformed and turbaned Indian doorman, for their well-known drink, the Singapore Sling. Inside, admiring the swirling wicker ceiling fans and antique furniture, we could imagine what it must have been like when Britain controlled Singapore.

My next stop was Bali, but since I had picked up some sort of intestinal virus, I was very tired at that point. Though I felt weak, I was strong enough to take a tour with a couple I had met on the beach in front of my hotel. We rented a car, hired a tour guide and drove all over the island, taking in the tiered rice paddies and the lush greenery. I was charmed by the local people, who seemed to relate to each other with the simplicity of children. In Bali children were taught music, dance, and various forms of art at an early age. We visited a shop where Balinese art was sold and I bought a beautifully carved, heavy wooden ball depicting a man in the lotus position with his hands covering his face. Next to the shop we could watch men sitting on woven mats as they practiced their skills in carving.

I was feeling weaker and was still unwell, so I changed my itinerary. Instead of going to Australia, I went to Hong Kong. I was feeling so sick I wondered if I should visit a doctor there, but instead decided to give up the effort to keep traveling. There is nothing worse than feeling awful so far away from home. I got on a plane bound for San Francisco after a stopover in Hawaii. Since I needed to go somewhere and rest, I tried unsuccessfully to reach my father by phone. When I arrived in San Francisco, I called my friend, Susan Moody, who had been my roommate in my Eastern Airlines training class. Fortunately she invited me to stay with her. Her husband was a doctor and he said I just needed to rest to rid my body of the Asian parasite I had contracted.

After this educational and colorful trip of six weeks, I transferred to New York City from Atlanta. I flew out of both La Guardia airport and JFK. I shared a large one-bedroom apartment with a flight attendant who flew with American Airlines. It worked out quite well for us. She was rarely in our apartment because she had family elsewhere and spent most of her time away. I was just so happy to be somewhere I could call home.

It was a dreadful time in my life. I knew Brent wanted to be with me, but at the same time he resented me. We were legally separated, which is a state of living in limbo. I began to develop serious emotional problems, so serious that I began thinking of suicide. I had a prescription for Valium and was planning to save a few months' supply to perform the deadly deed. I didn't have a clue what was really wrong with me and didn't realize the emotional lows were a result of my manic-depressive disease beginning to manifest. I did know I felt horrible about having to abandon my mother, and then being rejected by Brent. I was feeling depressed, quite hopeless and lonely. Since I was fortunate to have good medical insurance through the airlines, I did decide to see a good psychiatrist while I was living in New York City.

The female psychiatrist was a compassionate and enthusiastic Italian, who spent a good deal of time listening to me before scheduling me for a Rorschach test. After seeing my responses to the test, she concluded I was just suffering from reactive depression from the separation from Brent. He had been my anchor, despite my tendency to be a vagabond.

Even though I was depressed, I decided to end my limbo state by getting a divorce. Somehow I had the presence of mind to pull it all together in about three months. I went to the offices of the New York Supreme Court and found what I needed in their basement. I asked the clerk there for the files on uncontested divorces, since those files are a matter of public record. He probably thought I was a law student because he let me study them. I wrote down all the form numbers that were required, located the forms and then filled them out gradually. It took many visits to the clerk before I had everything in order. Sometimes the clerk would tell me what was wrong with my forms, other times I had to figure it out myself.

I had to hire an attorney for the final requirement, but rather than spend the money to have Brent served the papers, I asked him to come to New York and make it easier on both of us. He was pissed off at me for getting the divorce. I felt he had mixed feelings because he still cared, yet he was also losing control of someone whose life had revolved around his for the past seven years. We got drunk together and then went to the attorney's office to sign the final papers. I felt relieved when it was all over, and my depression started to dissipate.

8

Signs of Trouble

In the '70s, it seemed that everyone I knew was a drinker. I'm not sure how heavily other people drank, but at that time, I needed to drink, and I wanted to drink. A friend of mine said he noticed a personality change in me when I drank. I would become obnoxious and assertive, but I felt I deserved to drink any way I pleased and I proceeded to do just that!

Brent was working as a carpenter and living in Breckenridge, Colorado, while he waited to enter Case Western Reserve Medical School in Cleveland. He invited me to come skiing with him in February 1975 even though we were in the process of a divorce. One weekend we went skiing in Vail. It was late in the day when we took a break and split a bottle of wine. I then attempted to race Brent down the slopes and soon hit a large chunk of ice. Sprawled on the snow, I noticed a blinding pain in my right knee. Time seemed to stand still, and it stood still in a very bad way. I must have been in shock from ripping the ligament in my knee. Still intent on the race, Brent didn't realize I wasn't behind him until he had skied some distance, looked back to check on me, and saw me flat on my back surrounded by other skiers.

The ski patrol got me into a toboggan-like stretcher, took me down the mountain, put me into an ambulance, and took me to the emergency room of the local hospital. The doctor told me I would need surgery to reconstruct the torn ligaments. By this time, it was too late in the day to fill the prescription for codeine, so after we left the emergency room, Brent and I went to his favorite bar, and I was introduced to Tequila. I experienced self-medication for the first time in my drinking career. I drank heavily that night to alleviate my physical pain. The excruciating pain in my knee remains in my memory so clearly that I flinch anytime anyone or anything is near my knee.

I asked Brent to call Dr. Verne Chaney, the doctor I met in Nepal, who was located in New York City: Dr. Chaney knew a prominent knee specialist who had invented the artificial kneecap, and he recommended that I let this surgeon who practiced in New York City, perform the operation. I flew to New York as soon as I could get a flight and was admitted to the Hospital of special Surgery for total-ligament reconstruction and kneecap realignment. Afterward, I had to learn how to walk with a walker, then with crutches, and finally with a cane before the doctor would release me. After the surgery, Eagan Airlines put me on total disability and I spent the entire winter in a cast. I was still living with the American Airlines' flight attendant, but she had taken a leave of absence and was out of town.

The ordeal with my leg was frustrating because it was the first time in my life I was physically limited. I had been accustomed to racing around like a maniac and now had to accept that I must move slowly and cautiously. I was humbled and infuriated that I had to depend on the help of others. I was not easily accepting of my situation and for the first few months, I frequently lost my temper.

That spring I put my cane aside while I put my trash in the can outside my building and someone stole it. I decided it was a sign to start walking without my cane, even though it left me with a terribly vulnerable feeling. To this day, seeing someone struggling to get around with crutches or a cane brings back vivid memories for me.

I went to the Office of Vocational Rehabilitation that summer and after an evaluation, they arranged for me to study art. I had brought along all of my artwork from high school and college and from the time I had designed greeting cards for Rust Craft. They felt my presentation showed my artistic talent, and because of that I planned to attend Pratt Institute to study fine arts that fall.

When I began my classes at Pratt Institute, I drank only one or two glasses of wine in an evening, and sometimes none at all. I wasn't dating much and was totally immersed in creative expression. I was serious about the art foundation courses, which consisted of classes in drawing, form and space (which was mostly sculpture) and other artistically related courses. I wanted to excel and make the dean's list. I was thrilled to have accomplished the dean's list both semesters. If I had continued on this serious path, life certainly would have turned out differently for me.

At Christmas, my friend Leslie invited me to Nashville. I flew to Washington, D.C., to visit with my mother briefly and take her a Christmas gift, a porcelain hand-painted egg. My mother was sober and with eyes brimming her. Looking over with tears, she begged me to stay and celebrate Christmas with her. Looking back, I feel it was so cruel of me not to stay with her, but she had ruined too many of my holidays in the past with her drinking and insane behavior. I decided I could safely leave her alone and continued on to Nashville to celebrate Christmas with my friend and her family. It never occurred to me that I could trust my mother to remain sober and civil, even though she was sober that day and might have been throughout that year. My mother was living in a halfway house at the time and was probably in the fellowship of Alcoholics Anonymous. If I could redo anything in my life, I would have stayed to spend that Christmas with my mother. I think I could have gotten to know her and even learn to love her again. My decision to leave is the worst regret of my life.

While I was at Pratt, I took ballet lessons and the continual exercise built up my leg and made it stronger. Although I was by no means a dancer, the discipline of ballet was not only good for my leg, it meant diligence on my behalf. I was determined to succeed at something for once in my life!

Just before my thirtieth birthday in March 1976, through a friend I met Loni, who was searching for a roommate. We had dinner together and decided to try sharing an apartment. When we moved in together, she introduced me to a new approach to an evening out: we would go out "drinking." I was intrigued. The concept of making a night of drinking sounded like marvelous fun! But there was one drawback. I blacked out after three or four glasses of wine. I was told I was very funny and entertaining, but I couldn't remember all the fun I was supposed to be having. For an alcoholic, a blackout is a danger signal of worse things to come.

All my jet-set friends decided to rent a bus and celebrate all our friends' March birthdays on my birthday night. Marijuana joints were passed around the bus until everyone was stoned. Enjoying my marijuana high, I had decided not to drink and was delighted the next morning when I didn't have a hangover. The bus took us to a tiny restaurant in Chinatown. After the delicious Chinese delicacies, we had an ice cream birthday cake for dessert.

The following morning I was happy and sober when my mother called me. "Hi, Joni, I just wanted to tell you I tried to call on your birthday. I hope you forgive me for being a day late."

"That's OK, Mother, I was out having a great time. I'm meeting all sorts of new people and having lots of fun. I love my classes at Pratt and I'm making the grades for once in my life."

"You know I love you, Joni. Don't forget that."

"Sure, Mother. And I love you too." She sounded sober and I was happy for her.

"You're only going to be thirty once in your life. Kick up some dust while you are young. Honey, remember that I love you."

I didn't realize our conversation would be the last one I would ever have with my mother.

———————

Life was going very well for me; I was enjoying my classes and loved fitting into the New York scene. I was dating successful and powerful men and being driven to many places in limousines. Everything took an abrupt turn one night in the spring of 1976 when my Uncle Carl, my mother's youngest brother, called me from Galax, her hometown.

"Joni, do you have anyone nearby you can ask to be with you right now?"

"No, I don't." I was scared by the tone of his voice but Loni was out and I didn't know any of my new neighbors.

"I'm sorry, Joni, but I have to tell you your mother is dead. They found her in her Washington apartment."

Life stood still at that moment. I murmured a few pleasantries and hung up. I didn't have anyone I could call. Not knowing what else to do, I ran a bath and remember sitting in the bathtub watching my tears hit the water. I didn't know I was in shock. I felt so terribly alone and so wrong about everything. It was an extremely difficult night for me; I had so many regrets.

It was Pratt's end-of-term week, and I went to school the next morning to turn in some of my projects, then went to the airport and took the shuttle to Washington. My friend, Barry Colvert, an FBI agent who was Brent's closest friend and had known my mother, met me at the airport. Although I might have collapsed out of relief to see an old friend who could help me, I didn't feel as though I could relax and turn any of my concerns over to anyone else at that point. I had a terrible sense of guilt because I felt I had not given my mother a chance to prove her love for me, nor had I shown her my love. I felt that the previous Christmas would have been the test and I had chosen not to be with her. I had let her down.

Barry told me to try not to worry; he was there to help me. He drove me to the coroners office in downtown D.C., where my mothers body had been taken.

"Joni. I'm going to insist that I be the one to identify your mother. It wouldn't be easy for you to look at her. She's been dead for over two weeks and she's badly decomposed."

"But, Barry, she's my mother. I feel so horrible about this. I really need to see her," I protested.

"Trust me, Joni. I know that your mother would never want you to see her the way she looks right now." I had to trust him. If I had voiced more reluctance, Barry would have been insulted.

Mother had not told anyone what she was going to do and remained undiscovered until the stench reached the halls of the apartment house. They found my mother suffocated by a plastic bag she had placed over her head; she had even tied a tight ribbon around her neck and as an extra flourish had made a bow. Mother had been very dignified, ladylike and aloof when she was sober. The bow was a touch that only she would have added.

I accepted that the body in the morgue was my mother, and I signed all the necessary paperwork. In contemplating my mother's actions, I think she probably felt she hadn't given me the emotional support I needed in my life and was probably so depressed she gave up entirely. I felt that my mother had nothing material to give me for my thirtieth birthday, so she gave me her life. She had always stressed her greatest gift to herself was giving birth to me less than a month before she turned thirty in April 1946. I had been important to my mother—more so than I could have ever realized in my life at that time.

Barry drove me to her apartment. When I put the key in her door, I had the oddest sensation. I could smell roses and Mother hated roses. When her father died when she was ten years old, she told me there had been roses everywhere. Roses reminded her of death. The soft music she adored was playing on the radio in her room. She had an unbelievable "green thumb" and all her little plants were thriving—especially the Job's Tears I had given her. Her ironing board was up. The iron was unplugged, but her suitcases were packed. It was as if she had just stepped out for a while, a metaphysical mystery.

Barry took me to his home where his wife, Susan, a friend and fellow flight attendant, greeted me with open arms. All I wanted to do was drink, and they let me. The next day I met my fathers plane at Dulles Airport. He had flown in from San Francisco to help me with the funeral arrangements. His friend and Penn State college sweetheart, Cleo, met us at the airport and took us to the funeral home. I remember thinking how considerate it was for the funeral home to be open so late. Of course, now I realize that death is a twenty-four- hour situation. My father told me he would provide whatever funds were necessary and I could do anything I pleased. This was the first time in my life that my father gave me carte blanche for anything! I was filled with too much pain at the time to realize his generosity or even his own pain.

I sat in the funeral home surrounded by caskets of all prices, wondering what to do. Almost as if I were told what to do, I remembered my mother telling me years before that she wanted to be cremated. I looked tip and immediately saw a beautiful marble box with a lavender hue. In my heart, knew that it was to be the container for my mothers remains. As he promised, my father agreed with my choice.

I have forgotten most of the details because I was numb. To keep busy, I sorted and packed up all of my mothers clothing and personal effects. One incident stands out dearly. My father had come into my mothers bedroom, and while I was folding something he found a hinged, double-picture frame. On one side was a picture of my mother taken in Spain, and the other picture was of my father in his Naval uniform.

My father held it and started to cry. He slammed it shut so hard that the glass broke. "Why do you suppose people hurt each other so?" he asked poignantly. I had no answer to give him. At that moment I realized my father had loved my mother all these years, but they were just like oil and water— incompatible. Then there was the alcoholism, which just destroyed us completely.

My father and I flew to Roanoke, Virginia, and rented a car to drive to the little town of Galax. Dad did the best he could at taking charge. I just clutched the box containing my mothers ashes. The entire family was there, my Grannie Har-man and all of my mothers brothers and sisters. It would have been a good reunion except that both my father and I were devastated. My father played the role of surviving spouse, even though he had remarried, and no one dared question him. My father meant business when he took charge of any situation!

My father had already buried his second wife, Ysabel, in California. The two of them had been visiting Victoria, British Columbia, to celebrate his August birthday when the tragedy occurred. While they were standing on a sidewalk studying a restaurant menu, a young woman lost control of her Rambler station wagon and it jumped the curb and pinned Ysabel to the nearby building. Thinking fast, even though he had also been hit, my father got ten men in the vicinity to help lift the car away. It was no use; Ysabel had died in his arms shortly afterward. Deeply in love with Ysabel, my father had never recovered from this trauma, which was complicated by the Fact that he also had manic-depression. His mind started to go and his drinking escalated considerably. For years after he suffered from nightmares.

After the marble box was placed in the ground, my Aunt Evylee, who Was married to my Uncle Carl, placed a bouquet of violets, which were my mothers favorite flower, on top of the box. I was very touched by her gesture and followed her by taking a handful of soil to place on the box and my father followed. That was the only way I knew to close that chapter. It was a very windy day, and the wind blew my fathers tears across his face. I realized then he was all that I had in this world. He had been there to carry me through one of the most difficult phases of my life, and he was sober.

When we returned to my grandmothers house, it was filled with people. "How's Grannie taking it all?" I asked my Aunt Joyce, my mother's youngest sister. My grandmother was eighty-seven and going through chemotherapy.

"She has no idea what has happened," Joyce told me.

I walked over to Grannie and knelt to talk with her.

"Sister, do you grieve?" she asked me.

"Yes, Grannie," I replied.

"Then go. It is finished," she said.

Father and I then left. I had no idea those would be the last words my grandmother would ever speak to me.

After my mother's funeral, my drinking escalated. I was invited to Loni's summer house in the Hamptons on Long Island. She shared it with some co-workers from Wall Street. I met several young men there and was having the time of my life. I thought I was quite mature, unique, bright and beautiful at age thirty! I was petite and quite slender and my hair was almost to my waist. I was not a flirt; I didn't have to be. If the chemistry was right, I had a date. I had lots of dates! I was like a kid in a candy store and I felt like I was the kid with a million dollars to spend. Life was wonderful!

Frank was one of the men I met. I found him to be very original, especially since he chose not to drink. His substance of choice was marijuana. It didn't make him appear odd. It just made him mellow, easygoing and terribly funny. Pot made me totally incapacitated and gave me the "munchies." I couldn't even talk when I smoked; it was not physically possible. I just wanted anything wet and sweet. I sounded ridiculous when I said anything and there was no stopping me from trying to babble on senselessly. Eventually, I preferred to drink wine instead of smoking pot. I didn't like the feeling of losing total control.

———————⌘———————

In June, Uncle Carl called to tell me Grannie was dying and it was time for me to come to Galax to say goodbye to her. Uncle Carl picked me up at the airport and took me directly to the hospital. I didn't mean to cry, but when I leaned over to kiss Grannie, I could hear my tears hitting the rubber padding under her sheet.

Prior to my uncle's call, I had been scheduled to go to Miami for a physical examination by the doctor at the Eastern Airlines Medical Department. I was hoping to be cleared by the doctor so I could return to my flying status. I had not flown since my leg injury in February 1975, and it was now June of 1976. My Aunt Joyce insisted I leave immediately for Miami and take care of this situation. There was no arguing with her, so I flew to Miami. That night when I called Uncle Carl for an update, he told me Grannie had died a few minutes after I left. I called my supervisor and received emergency status passes to return to Virginia. Grannie had a beautiful ceremony and funeral. I was so relieved that she no longer had to suffer the pain of bone cancer.

I was able to return to flying, but I didn't have the same enthusiasm because I was suffering from depression. In those early days of my illness, I wasn't sad when depression hit me; my thinking would lack clarity and I would be exhausted from the lack of physical energy and stamina.

It wasn't easy to work out a daily flying schedule and manage to get the weekends off so that I could still go to the Hamptons. Loni had decided to get her own apartment, and I couldn't afford the two-bedroom apartment alone. Some friends, David and his wife Sherry, were expecting their first baby, had just moved to New York and were looking for an apartment with two bedrooms. Fortunately, they sublet my apartment. My friend, Frank, came to my rescue when he invited me to share his apartment.

I was a very independent person when I moved in with Frank, but my independence caused us problems. Frank had his version of how life should be lived and, of course, I had mine! Since it was a platonic arrangement, we encouraged each other to date. But jealousy erupted between us. Each of us hated it when the other spent the night away or went out on a date.

Frank was the first person to tell me I was an alcoholic. I claimed I wasn't. I could go a day without wine, but I was in denial. I demanded to have things my way. I didn't know then that alcoholics are very self-centered, self-absorbed, selfish people. I was all of that, as were my parents and most of my alcoholic family and friends.

After Labor Day I went for a routine gynecological exam and found out I had an unusual lump in my abdomen. Because of a possible malignancy, the doctor admitted me to Roosevelt Hospital for exploratory surgery in October. The night before my surgery, I asked the doctor what would be the worst thing that could happen. He told me that if I had ovarian cancer, I would Probably have less than six months to live.

That night, as I lay in my bed looking out at the lights of New York City, I finally saw things realistically. Now and then things that occur to us are like a wake-up call and are meant to jolt us into awareness. I was thirty years old and I hadn't accomplished much of anything. I had been in the hospital for over a week waiting for each of the different test results and for news of whether I needed surgery. All of the jet-setters I had been hanging around with just disappeared. Only my father and a few friends were still in the picture. I thought how it was so true that in hard times you find out who your real friends are. All I could think of was leaving New York City and going somewhere I felt safe and comfortable. I reflected on the many places I had traveled and lived and realized I didn't belong anywhere. I had absolutely no roots. I wasn't depressed about dying; I just felt cornered, lost, sad and fearful more than depressed. It was a very frustrating and lonely feeling.

I realized how unhappy I was in New York and how shallow my existence was at that time in my life. Something had to change, but I wondered where I should go. I remembered how happy my mother and I had been on the day we had explored the island of Maui. Although my mother was gone, I could return to those cliffs and relive the experience I had had with her, but I knew I was a city person and Hana, Hawaii, was very remote. Besides, many people had insisted that once I'd lived in Manhattan, I could never successfully move away from that city. They told me I'd always have the urge to return to the hustle and bustle. Whatever I decided, I was definitely sure, despite the advice to the contrary, that I wanted out of this city.

My surgery was performed at seven in the morning, and late that afternoon I regained consciousness. My friend Leslie was there when I woke up. The doctor came in to tell me he had removed a large, benign tumor. He said I would be fine eventually and emphasized the importance of taking it easy while I gave my body time to heal.

Later, my friends Tony, Lucy and Frank arrived to support me. Frank, who is tall already, was wearing his cowboy hat. At my door a nurse stopped him. "You can only visit if you are family," she told him firmly.

"I am family," he growled at her convincingly. She didn't dare dispute him.

Not long afterward, my father stormed in, late as usual. He took a look at Tony and Lucy and asked me in his superior tone, "How do those two fit in?"

"They're friends, of course," I said to him groggily. I pointed at each of them, "That's Tony, that's Lucy, and Frank's wearing the cowboy hat." I was grateful that most of my friends had a sense of humor. No one took my father seriously, even when he was acting like a jerk. Because he was used to being the center of attention, he always seemed to dislike most of my friends. Dad had the knack of pissing people off and had always been that way. I was heavily sedated and couldn't see clearly, but I knew the scene was amusing.

I felt grateful to have such a colorful assortment of friends and "family," many of them from other countries. Tony was Italian and Lucy came from Puerto Rico, for instance. I fell asleep with a sense of peace. It was a relief to know I had more than six months to rectify my life. The urgency to move to Hawaii dissipated.

By Christmas, Frank and I were intimately involved. We declared a ceasefire—I didn't pick on him and he no longer insisted I face up to the fact that I was an alcoholic. Frank and I had a great deal of fun together. He had a quick temper, and I was not playing with a full deck, but somehow we met in the middle and managed to have a good time. My Christmas with Frank that year was the happiest Christmas I had had since the ones I spent with Brent.

Frank was very good to me. We had the same sense of humor and we liked the same things: the same food, music and people. He loved to play his guitar for me. Frank took me out often to share all the wonderful things the city had to offer, and I enjoyed his company. Despite the love and security that Frank gave me, I just couldn't remain in New York. At that time I wasn't capable of being cherished; I wouldn't have recognized love if God Himself had come down to try to explain it to me! I was in total denial of being of any value.

By the winter of 1977, I could no longer stand the noise and rush of the city. One snowy morning the sanitation department made such a racket I called a friend in the car business to ask him to take me to Connecticut where I bought a cat I drove out to Long Island and rented a three-bedroom beach house in East Hampton. It was winter and the rent was very low. I loved the solitude and the peace as I drove back and forth from Kennedy International Airport, about a two-hour drive each way. I really needed solitude after the noise and commotion of the city. After my flights I would buy a jug of wine and an artificial log to burn in the large fireplace in my living room.

On a cold morning in March, I took off for Martinique; I wanted to celebrate my birthday where it was warm and I could swim. Walter was one of the interesting people I met, and he chartered a sailboat one afternoon and invited me to join him and some of his friends. We anchored off a tiny village in a breathtaking cove and went by dinghy to a small restaurant on the beach. This was my first opportunity to eat Caribbean cuisine, and I loved it. I enjoyed the islands and the tropical temperature so much I decided to request a transfer to our Miami base.

In September that year I bought a condominium in Fort Lauderdale in a complex located on a private island. It was a lovely, spacious, two-bedroom home on the fifth floor with a spectacular view of the winding New River and the western sky with its beautiful sunsets.

Brent came to visit me during the summer of 1978 when he was in his final year of medical school. We had been separated for four years and divorced for two years, but he asked me to marry him again. He didn't know where he would be practicing medicine or exactly where he wanted to live; since the Navy had paid for most of his tuition, he owed them time.

We drank heavily during his visit, but we had a romantic and enjoyable time together because we were still very fond of each other. If we married we would have to move where the Navy sent him, but I was quite happy with my home in Florida. However, the last night we were together, we had a heated argument. To this day, I can't remember what the argument was about, but he left and that was the last I ever saw of him. I do remember we were both very drunk.

Shortly after he had annulment papers drawn up. Our marriage was to be considered null and void in the eyes of the Roman Catholic Church. In August 1979, Brent was remarried in the Roman Catholic Church to a very young Catholic woman.

When Brent stepped completely out of my life that summer, two other men, Bob and David, both of whom I had dated previously, asked me to marry them. At that time married life didn't really suit me, and I turned them down. David, who I'd met in Barcelona in 1969, had been Brent's shipmate and was still married when he asked me. He and his wife had sublet my New York apartment not long before, and I thought his mind had slipped since his wife had just given birth to a son. He came to Fort Lauderdale unannounced and expected that I would just drop everything and marry him.

I had been so seriously hurt by Brent that the thought of another marriage commitment scared me. I did not have any idea of what marriage entailed and I still felt like I was living in limbo. I led a bizarre lifestyle— drinking, flying and caring for no one but myself. I had no depth to my personality. I was just coasting through life leading an empty existence. I was like a surfer riding the waves of life with a liter of wine under each arm. Each wave that I rode was, in essence, just another emotional crisis.

I had joined the Gulf Stream Sailing Club in August 1979 and met several new friends. Harvey, an assistant district attorney, was bright, witty, and funny. The only problem we had was my drinking. Being very conscious of his own health, he had great difficulty accepting it, and it caused us terrible problems. He could see potential in me and it hurt him to see me trying to self-destruct. Since I was an alcoholic, I didn't understand why he just didn't take a drink and forget about it.

When one drinking incident occurred at my condo complex, I should have seen my insanity. A group of us at the complex drank together, ate together, went places together, and partied together. Valerie, who was British and one of the gals in the group, had a party to celebrate her fortieth birthday. She made a potent brew for it called cold tea, a mixture of rum, vodka and lime juice. Harvey had to work late that night, so I went to the party with my roommate, Susie. We all drank a lot of cold tea and then crammed together on a lounge chair to have our picture taken. I fell off the lounge chair and cut open my jaw and cheek bone. It didn't appear to me to be much of cut, so I went up to my condo, sprayed my face with Bactine and returned to the party. When Harvey arrived later and saw the cut, he was horrified and immediately took me to the emergency room. We had a terrible fight when he brought me home, and he left.

The next morning when I woke up, I saw Susie with a huge welt on her nose and two black eyes. She had been swimming in the pool the previous night without her contacts and had misjudged her distance. She had broken her nose on the edge of the pool. I looked pretty bad myself. We decided to get some breakfast, somewhere that no one would know us. We went to Lester's Diner and while we were eating, a huge truck driver came up to our table and asked us, "Which one of you sweet little ladies won?" We looked at each other and realized we were a pitiful sight. I guess it was funny, but we felt too terrible to laugh. So much for Valerie's cold tea!

During the fall of 1979, I flew out of Miami International Airport to most of the Caribbean islands. On one flight, during hurricane David, we hit serious turbulence and another flight attendant and I were injured. She was put in the pain unit at Jackson Memorial Hospital, with back injuries. She never recovered. I was put in traction in a hospital in Fort Lauderdale due to a back injury. I stayed in the hospital for over two weeks. The doctor thought I was fine, but time would prove that the injury was significant.

During this period of my life, my drinking escalated. I was basically out of control when I drank.

9

My Father's Death

Christmas of 1979 at my Fort Lauderdale condo was very memorable— it was the last Christmas my father and I spent together. My father really struggled to stay sober, but I found it very difficult to accept the fact that he couldn't stop drinking. It never occurred to me that we both suffered the same problem! One afternoon, my father borrowed my TV antenna and rigged himself a fishing rod. From my balcony I could see him sitting on the sea wall fishing down by the river. He would look one way and then the other and then reach inside a bag, take out a beer, and sneak a drink. I felt a sense of pity for him because it seemed such an innocent attempt at enjoying himself. I also realized he was lonely. My father had never recovered from Ysabel's tragic death.

I regret now that I didn't go down and join him for a beer, but I didn't know he wouldn't be around for another Christmas. Because of my past experience, I now tell the people I love just how important they are to me. I do that as often as I can because I don't know when my last chance to express my love will be.

I went to stay with my father in San Francisco for a week in May 1980. He was teaching his usual summer course in mosaic techniques at the California College of Arts and Crafts. We spent every day together in his studio. He would teach his students and I would paint. Dad would make suggestions about the colors I should use and give me other advice. Everything was perfect that week.

"You know, Jon, I'm really very proud of you and your accomplishments," my father told me one day when we went to lunch together.

I was quite surprised. It was the acceptance and approval I had yearned for. and I mumbled, "Thank you, Dad, I appreciate that."

"I guess I didn't have the faith in you I should have had, Jon. You've been a flight attendant with Eastern Airlines now for twelve years and certainly proved you aren't a bum." I looked at him with tears welling up, not able to say anything. He continued, "I want to share a dream of mine. I really want to open an art institute in Chimayo, New Mexico, and I'd just love it if you'd think about quitting your job with Eastern and help me start the school. We'd be able to spend time together doing what we both love."

"That's a great idea, Dad. I'm sure it's just what you need to do. But flying's been my lift for so long and I really enjoy it. Even though I'd hate to quit, I'm going to seriously think about your idea," I said enthusiastically, but I honestly didn't think I could give up the only security I had ever known, my work with Eastern Airlines. "But what about Daisy?" I asked. She was a woman he was currently dating.

"I think the relationship has run its course. Besides I want to move to New Mexico and get the art school off the ground, something Daisy is not interested in."

I had managed to get the entire month of June and July off that year and decided I would use this time to drive to New Mexico and investigate the village of Chimayo, which had so enchanted my father.

My first stop was New Orleans, where I visited Allen, an attorney friend of my old Fort Lauderdale boyfriend, Harvey. I didn't realize until afterward that Harvey had suggested I get together with Allen because we were both lushes. Nevertheless, I had a fabulous time with Allen. He was tall and very distinguished in his three-piece suit, and was bright and extremely funny. He showed me the town, introduced me to an assortment of people, and took me to various parties. We went to shrimp boils, oyster parties and heard lots of jazz. If there wasn't a party, we made one. New Orleans was my kind of town!

After leaving the Big Easy, I remember how beautiful the hills looked as I approached Santa Fe at dawn. Just as the sun was rising, I was blessed to find a secondary road instead of the interstate highway. It was as if the scene were all in slow motion. I found a terrific Spanish-style hotel right in the center of Santa Fe, and I went right to bed and slept soundly until late afternoon. When I got up, I went out to explore the town. I walked along the river and came across a group of people playing Frisbee.

We talked and they invited me to join them for a meal at a Mexican restaurant. I met a very nice man, and after too many margaritas, I think we might have gotten engaged. I'm not exactly clear about what happened, but I ended up staying with him for a few days. A very charming man with lots of interesting tales to tell, he was a geologist for an oil company. Since he was leaving to do some camping with his friends on horseback, he invited me to me to visit him again. I really liked him, so I told him that I would be in touch.

The sleepy little village of Chimayo was unusual and Far off the beaten path. Most of the villagers spoke to each other in Spanish and few people spoke English. I found a tiny church called El Sanctuario. Near the chapel a small dirt pit was considered holy. Crutches lined the walls of the room next to the pit, and many framed letters were displayed from people who claimed to have been healed there. I could see why my father had been charmed by the area. With his talent and background, I think he would have made a success of an art school if he had lived. I have since visited the charming town and concluded I would have enjoyed living there and teaching art to gifted students.

I continued on to Ranchos de Taos to visit friends. I had never visited these people in their new home, and I was amazed that it was an authentically restored hacienda. While I was there, I called my father and found out he had married Daisy, the lady he told me he was no longer going to see. I wondered about his plan to open the art school, but I let it go. That was enough information for an afternoon.

My roommate Susie and I had made plans to meet at the Aspen, Colorado airport, so I continued north into Colorado to meet her flight. We stayed in Aspen for a few nights then continued to Crested Butte, Colorado, to stay with some of her friends from college. This was my first experience at "jeeping." One day we took the jeep up a dried creek to a mountain called the Red Lady. We stopped to have a picnic way up past the timberline where there were still banks of snow. We cooled our wine and champagne in the snow banks and even played in the snow. I tried to ski down a bank barefooted, which was amusing but not very effective! The wildlife—deer, rabbits, chipmunks and birds, curiously observed us, seemingly unafraid. It had been a long time since I had been in a mountain setting in the summer, and the view was absolutely spectacular. We saw waterfalls and lakes that were so beautiful it took my breath away.

Susie and I continued our vacation by driving on to Telluride and then over to Durango, where we stopped to drink margaritas. We were obviously looking very young since the barmaid asked to see our identification. I was thirty-four, so that boosted my ego! Susie and I decided to drive back w Albuquerque, New Mexico. She wanted to fly back to Florida to spend some of her vacation with her family, and I wanted to return to Fort Lauderdale.

When I got home, Susie and some of our neighbor pals were planning a dinner party by the pool for that evening. Everyone was asked to bring something. During the early stages of the party I had to return to the apartment for something. Susie came up to help me, and I was surprised that when the phone rang she answered it. She stood there dazed as she handed my phone to me. Daisy s son, my new stepbrother announced, "Your father is dead."

I literally collapsed. I fell on my bad knee and dislocated it. The pain from my knee combined with the news of my Ethers death was devastating and I wailed like an animal. Susie was shocked because she loved my Ether as well. She took me in her arms and held me while I sobbed hysterically and our tears intermingled. It didn't take long before all our friends had gathered in our apartment. Everyone was there for me and it touched my heart since I had not had this kind of support when my mother died. I don't remember much more because the spirits I had imbibed were slowly taking effect. For the first time in my life, I was encouraged to drink.

Every one of my friends and neighbors had liked my father. Despite our painful history, I could appreciate the fact that my father was a genuine character, if there ever was one. He is one of the reasons I am writing this story. I had often begged him to write his own life story, but he would always tell me he would do that for me in the year 2001, since he was too busy with his own life! Because of his many plans and ideas, he told me there would never be enough time for him to stop and write until then. He had lived in sixty-four countries and had tales to tell about all of them.

My Ether had been my rock and I loved him despite everything. Oftentimes I hated him because of his alcohol abuse. He seemed to go out of his way to embarrass me. However, he was so lovable at times that it was difficult for me to stay angry with him. My rugged handsome father had been so good-looking and majestic, even at seventy. I knew he was proud of me and when he was sober he tried to give me encouragement. He had always reminded me I was from good stock and I should amount to something. My father was always laughing and had an outrageously funny sense of humor. He told me that as I grew older, I would see the value of a good companion. I had asked so little of my Ether in his lifetime. I think that bothered him, or possibly it pleased him. I will never know the answer.

I remembered all his accomplishments. He had been a talented landscape artist, a mosaic artist, an engineer and watercolorist. He was bright, generous, good-natured, and never without energy or enthusiasm when he was sober. He had been a firm believer in eating the right foods and getting plenty of rest and exercise (he had just left alcohol out of the equation). Now all I had left of him was his paintings, watercolors and a few mosaic pieces. Losing my father so suddenly was the most traumatic thing that had ever happened to me. It was worse than losing my mother because he and I had built a bond between us during his last few years. At that time I felt as if someone had taken a large jigsaw puzzle and thrown it up into the wind. It was my destiny to find all those pieces and to slowly put them all back together again—one piece at a time.

Susie accompanied me to San Francisco. My new stepbrother, Steve, didn't want to see me and refused to let me use Daisy's car. However, he did arrange for Susie and me to have access to her home, which my Ether and Daisy had shared in Walnut Creek. Once we were situated, we rented a car and Susie drove because of my re-injured knee. We went to the coroner's office, and I tried to have my Ether's body released to me since I wanted to have his funeral on the East Coast, where his high school and college friends lived. However, I was no longer considered the next-of-kin, due to his recent marriage to Daisy.

Daisy was onboard a Norwegian ship cruising the waters off the coast of Scandinavia. I recalled the conversation I had had with my father in May. He told me she planned to go on a cruise in July and that she had excluded him. I believe he may have married her in July since he didn't want to be left alone and was hoping she would not go. Regardless of who was offended, I was in California, she was somewhere in the North Sea, and my father was in the morgue. I was having great difficulty with my attempts to get his body to a funeral home. The coroner sent at least four cables to Daisy, requesting that she authorize the release of my Ether's body to me, his daughter. There seemed to be a language barrier or something else wrong, even though I was sure she was also very upset. My new stepmother kept sending cables about having a great time and that VA burial benefits were okay with her. There were several bizarre messages.

Finally the coroner agreed to release my fathers body so I could begin the procedure of getting him buried in Virginia, as he had requested of me years ago. His death was attributed to his alcohol abuse. Not too long before he died, my Ether had attended a treatment center for alcohol rehabilitation in Seattle. Obviously it didn't take. My father was a Roman Catholic, so I went to a Catholic priest and asked him if there was any way he could approve a cremation, since cremation had been forbidden by the Catholic Church for centuries. Thankfully, I received his approval for cremation, so I went to the funeral home and told the director to make the necessary arrangements and to send the ashes to the funeral home in Virginia.

On my flight to the East Coast, I wondered why I hadn't been given my father's rings, which included his class ring from Penn State, or his favorite necklace. He had always worn a little silver fish on a chain to symbolize his Christianity; in the middle of the fish was a small cross. I had too much to think about. In addition to the emotional upheaval, there were all the legalities to deal with, like the absence of a will. Everything seemed to be in a terrible state. Because of the crisis, I was drinking more heavily than ever and, of course, that clouded my judgment and actions.

The funeral parlor in California sent the ashes to the funeral home in Virginia, but the ashes got lost on the way. This problem held up the funeral. All the friends, family and neighbors, who had planned to drop everything to my father's funeral, had to continue with their lives. My knee was getting worse and very swollen and I was in great pain. I was encouraged to leave for New York and have more surgery on it since we did not know when my father's ashes would arrive. After the surgery, I was very dopey when I came to, but I called my aunt. She told me that my father's ashes had arrived that morning and that a few Emily members and friends had had a graveside service that day and buried my father's remains. It seemed like such an insignificant ending to such a tremendous life. I felt very sad and hurt that I had been excluded from the service. It would have given me the opportunity to say a proper goodbye.

At that time, I didn't feel any closure with my Ether. It was still so difficult to believe he was dead. It was as if it had all been a bad dream. Somehow, I felt I might get a postcard or a phone call from him telling me it had all been a mistake. I would not have been surprised if he had walked into my hospital room with an explanation. It was very difficult to deal with life without him. and it took me well over fifteen years to learn how to deal with the loss. I felt my strength drained from me after I realized this was by no means a dream. His death left a hole in my soul.

When my stepmother came home from her cruise, I flew out to California to ask why she had left my father so soon after the fourth of July, when they had gotten married. July 4'h is a deadly omen for me because both my Ethers parents died on that date, and my fathers own death was shortly after that fateful day. I wondered why he had picked it as his marriage date.

I also wanted to see if she had kept his will, which I planned to contest if he had left her very much because I was disappointed in and angry with her. She told me she was having their marriage annulled, and I was to take all of my Ethers possessions out of her house as soon as possible. This became a living nightmare since my Ether kept all of his paperwork under the bed in Paper bags! He had saved literally everything. The paperwork mess was the worst chaos I had ever experienced! I felt ridiculous, but I took the jumble of papers to an attorney in downtown San Francisco, who wasn't fazed one bit! After sorting through it all, he told me it would take at least eighteen months to settle the estate.

I had never driven a truck before, but Daisy arranged to loan one to me so could haul away my father's clothes. I took them into the Mission District of San Francisco and donated them to a men's alcoholic recovery house. His other possessions were in a storage unit many miles from

Walnut Creek. When I contacted the storage unit manager, I was told it was urgent that I remove all the contents as soon as possible. The lease had expired and they were ready to auction off the contents. They gave me twenty-four hours to take what I wanted. I went to the storage unit in the loaned truck and was horrified when I opened the unit—my father had saved everything in his seventy years! The unit was stacked to the brim. I didn't know where to begin, what to save or what to discard. It was a challenge trying to decide what to do. I had no idea what was important and what was just sentimental. I made several trips to the city dump with the truck piled high. I felt guilty for having so little use for my father's earthly treasures, and it bothers me to this day.

Daisy and I were as civil to each other as we could possibly be. When I was nearly finished, she asked me to take my father's car with me as soon as possible to free up her guest parking spot. I left in my fathers Pinto (he was always frugal in his choice of cars) the Sunday morning of Labor Day weekend before the sun came up and headed for Los Angeles to visit my friend Leslie for a few days of rest. Since I was not familiar with a stick shift, I only stopped for gas along the way. I lurched every time I started the engine and while trying to return to the freeway. I was grateful there weren't many people to witness my hopping out of one gas station after another.

From Leslie's, I headed east to Las Vegas. The sun was setting as I approached. Slowly the neon lights came on, and by the time I arrived, the city was lit up like a huge, gaudy birthday cake. There seemed to be zillions of lights. I checked into a well-known hotel in the center of everything. Since I had my airline employee ID, I was given a considerable discount, and my room turned out to be a magnificent suite! Everything that I had ever heard about Las Vegas was true. The town never sleeps and it is filled with all sorts of characters. I wandered around until late and went to see a comedian perform. Las Vegas was a fascinating place. It glittered with excitement and took my mind off all my worries. I didn't think about drinking because I was too busy exploring Vegas.

My next destination was the Grand Canyon. I had never seen it from the ground, although I'd passed over it many times by plane. I had been drinking wine and continued to drive, which led to poor judgment. I ended up in a ditch in the middle of the night. Fortunately, a forest ranger and h's girlfriend, who were on their way to a party, found me unhurt, lie helped me get my car out of the ditch and invited me to the party. I joined them; drinking tequila shooters and spent a restful night in my sleeping bag on floor of their trailer. The next morning, I woke up rested and anxious to see the Grand Canyon.

When I walked to the edge of the canyon and saw the immense depth and scope of it, I wanted to spend weeks exploring this deep and mysterious place! I didn't have the time to explore, so I took a helicopter ride over and around the canyon. It was one of the most electrifying things I've done in my life. As the chopper left the solid ground and went over the canyon, I squealed in terror and delight when the earth dropped hundreds of feet beneath us. What a memorable, spectacular sight to behold!

I headed up to Crested Butte, Colorado, to retrieve my car I had left at the Denver airport earlier in the summer. I felt there would be some semblance of order in my life if I could get both my car and my father's car in the same place. I wanted to sell them and buy a jeep.

The next morning I took a flight to Denver on a small aircraft. After the flight landed in Denver, the pilot, a man named Keith who lived in Gunnison, Colorado, asked me if I'd like to have a Coke with him. I said I'd prefer a Bloody Mary. We went to the bar and chatted for awhile, and he asked if I would like to join him for dinner that night. I didn't know it, but that was the beginning of my second marriage. We had known each other less than two months when we were married in November of 1980 in Fort Lauderdale at the Church by the Sea. When we returned to Colorado to live in his home, I discovered I could only tolerate him and the living conditions in Gunnison, Colorado, for six weeks. He took me to a priest to find out why I was being so difficult and why I drank until I passed out. He didn't understand alcoholism, and I wasn't ready to quit drinking. Keith couldn't stand my drinking and I couldn't stop drinking. I returned to the East Coast and my home in Fort Lauderdale, and shortly afterward he came to live with me in Florida during the winter and got a job as a pilot for a private company.

Deciding to get my body and my mind into better shape, I went to an ashram in Calabasas, California, for a week. The routine consisted of abstinence from alcohol, nicotine, caffeine, dairy products, sugar and meat. I handled the discipline and felt I had a handle on my life when I left the ashram. Keith was doing some crop dusting in South Dakota and

I went directly from the ashram to be with him. Right away he took me to a bar so he could be with his friends and watch a football game.

I sat at the bar with all the alcohol staring back at me. I didn't know where to go or what to do, so eventually I ordered a drink. At the ashram they had encouraged us to walk a mile a day and I asked Keith if he could get a hotel room on the outskirts of town so I could walk in the country. We were there for about three days before he complained about the carpool situation with the other pilots. That was the end of being in the country We went back to the tiny motel downtown, and it put me in a depression. My trip to South Dakota was insightful because I could see that the marriage was not going anywhere.

Keith was concerned about me and about my behavior when I was drunk. He told me he just wanted me to be well and sober. As my mood swings became stronger and more obvious, he insisted I seek psychiatric help, which I did. I began to need hospitalization for depressive states. I went from psychiatrist to psychiatrist hoping to hear something besides my need to join Alcoholics Anonymous! I went to a treatment center for alcoholism, but while I was there, I just could not admit that I was an alcoholic. After nineteen days, I was still in denial. The treatment center said it was no use for me to stay if I was going to continue with my denial. I could not admit nor accept the fact I was an alcoholic.

Keith and I were divorced in 1982. Because of my mental state, we were simply not compatible. I had bought a thirty-seven-foot fiberglass sailboat and Keith ended up living on it for awhile after he moved out. I know I was at fault for the demise of our marriage because I was a difficult drunk. Sobriety is a gift from God. Obviously, I wasn't ready to ask for this gift.

I was desperate to find someone to love me, despite my alcoholism. Bill came into my life. I was so relieved that he seemed to care for me and that he didn't have the need to change me. Physically, he reminded me of my first husband, Brent. He was tall, well-built, dark-haired and very handsome. Just like Brent, he was an alcoholic. Of course Bill and I got along famously—we drank our brains out and stumbled around through life together!

I was drinking too much and working too hard—burning the candle at both ends. During a transcontinental flight, I began to hemorrhage.

I was taken off my flights for the next month and was supposed to rest. The bleeding, however, became a serious problem. The more I drank, the worse it became, and the worse the bleeding got, the more I drank. The condition got so bad I had to undergo a hysterectomy in October 1983.

Bill came to see me once while I was in the hospital. He was so drunk he fell over my IV pole. He never returned. There I was in the hospital, abandoned by my boyfriend. I became so seriously depressed that my attending physician called in two psychiatrists to talk with me so they could evaluate whether I would be able to withstand the surgery They felt positive enough about me that the operation was performed. When I was discharged from the hospital, Bill sent his father to pick me up and take me home. Too weak and too confused to think clearly, I felt like all these problems were my fault and I fell into a deeper depression. I was fortunate that my physician and my psychiatrist arranged for a nurse to be at my home to assist me when I arrived. It was the third Christmas following my father's death and it was a bleak and lonely one.

When the estate was settled, I had inherited a considerable amount of money from my father. But three years later, after I had bought the sailboat, I had used up most of the money. My best friends had given up on me; not a soul was willing to support me. I was totally alone.

David, the man who, with his family, had sublet my New York apartment almost ten years before, had asked me to be his mistress many years ago, but I had never considered it until that lonely Christmas season. I felt I had nothing to lose. Some company was better than none. In January 1984, I called David and consented to have a life with him on his terms. We planned a rendezvous in New York. I decided that this time I wouldn't feel anything romantically again—NOT EVER!

My way had been all wrong, and I was slowly running out of money. I was on long-term disability from the airlines due to my depression. I had sold my father's house to pay cash for the sailboat and the rarely used boat sat tied up at the dock. I paid for the dockage—month after month.

10

Things Fall Apart

I needed to be needed, and David seemed to be the missing piece in my life at that time. He declared he wanted me, and that he was going to call the shots. I didn't fight him. I couldn't. I was finished with trying to have things my way. I was limp and almost lifeless. I was defeated. I turned myself over to David completely.

One morning, while David was at work, I started out to go to the hair salon to get refurbished from head to toe. When I stepped outside into the cold January air of New York, I couldn't move any further. It was as if I was frozen onto the sidewalk. I couldn't even make it to the curb to catch a taxi. Ordinarily, there would have been a doorman to assist me, but I was alone. I inched back to the building and put my back up against the wall. The whole of New York City swirled around me. For a short period, I thought I was going to pass out. I held onto the building with my hands and fingers, feeling intense and terrifying fear. I knew if I inched along, I could walk slowly down Fifth Avenue. Despite the freezing wind, the perspiration flowed off me and soaked my clothing. I held my fur jacket open to let the wind cool me off. This, as I discovered later, was my first panic attack. It was immobilizing, but somehow I managed to slowly walk the twenty blocks to the salon. I was late but I made it for my appointment. I had my hair styled and had a pedicure and manicure. Most women would adore this opportunity, but it was everything I could do to keep from crying. David had me where he wanted me. He had me, but I no longer had myself and my freedom. He made it perfectly clear that this was a relationship based on lust. My spirit was broken.

The next day my friend Terri joined me for lunch at a very posh restaurant in the hotel where David and I were staying. We were both beautiful, polished and well-dressed and looked the part of well-bred society. We ordered champagne, but neither of us could pick up the glasses. We were both suffering from the shakes that accompany alcoholism. We didn't need to explain anything to each other. In unison, we ordered strong screwdrivers. Waiting for the inevitable buzz and an eventual lull in the shakes, we drank several. Once that happened, we were on a roll. We laughed and chatted until we were so drunk we began to forget what we were talking about.

Terri had to come up with me to the hotel room so we could sleep it off until David returned from work that day. By the time he arrived it was "happy hour" and time to start over. David never seemed to mind my drinking and joined Terri and me to get a brand new start. New York was just too fast-paced for me, so it was a relief when David left to return to his family on the West Coast and I went back to Fort Lauderdale.

On this particular trip home, I stopped off in Nassau in the Bahamas to see my friend, Valerie. She had been my neighbor for several years in Fort Lauderdale. Valerie met my flight and off we went. It was exciting to drive on the left, which I hadn't done in a very long time. We drove up a road that cut through a rock and led down to the sea. When I saw the brilliant turquoise color of the water, I immediately fell in love with the Bahamas! That night I called David and told him I had decided to sell my condominium in Fort Lauderdale and move to Nassau. David groaned. He liked things the way they were. By the end of March, I had sold my condominium and most of my furniture and had moved into an apartment on Love Beach, twenty miles from downtown Nassau.

I needed to get my boat to the Bahamas and located a licensed sea captain. I asked her to help me get things in order and prepare to move my boat to the Bahamas from Fort Lauderdale. Since I needed to outfit the boar, David gave me the money. I also decided to have a lot of carpentry work done and to change the refrigeration around. It all cost over $20,000.

My urge to overspend is a result of my manic-depressive bipolar disorder. The surges of irrational thinking accompanied by intense energy and the urge to spend money became more prevalent, but in those days I masked this awareness with alcohol. Of course, what goes up must come down, so I would go crashing into a depression and mask that as well with denial and drinking. All I knew about myself was that I was different. It has taken a great deal of time to realize that manic-depression is a chemical imbalance and that I had needed medication for this disorder all along. Lithium, the best known medication for bipolar disorder, is washed out of the system with alcohol. I needed to stop drinking.

Between February and May 1984, I was in a manic state. Much of my behavior was disguised at the time by my heavy drinking. However, the energy I spent served a purpose. I was able to get my important belongings and some

furniture into storage. I got my car and a small amount of furniture shipped to the Bahamas before my boat was ready for the crossing to Nassau.

My depression hit me when it was time to make the crossing. Depressions, for me, don't necessarily mean I get sad. I just cannot function. It's as if my brain shuts down, my energy level is nil, and I become disoriented.

No one at that time was around me long enough to make observations and confront me about my behavior. I needed someone to tell me how my actions appeared to them. I had no earthly idea how bizarrely I acted. I was always sedating my behavior with too much alcohol. However, at either extreme, I now know it must have been difficult for those who attempted to cope with me. That's why there was so much distance between me and the people I came in contact with daily. Like most active alcoholics, I didn't know how to listen, thus I didn't hear.

Now I know that the distance had been created long, long ago during my formative years as a young girl. I had risked being close to my husband, Brent, and that had backfired on me.

11

The Bahamas and Onward

Now that I was living in another country, life became simple and serene. I had my dear cat, Penelope, and everything I needed was at my fingertips. The switchboard for the apartment complex would only take incoming calls, and I told my landlady each day just whose calls I would accept. David was probably the only one who knew the phone number, so that worked out well. I did not have a TV my cassette player was broken, and I was in such a remote location, in the center of a quiet coconut grove, I couldn't get a radio station. That was fine with me. I learned to live with silence and the distant sound of the surf.

I met Rosemary, a wonderful Bahamian neighbor who was tolerant of me, because, as she put it, I "had a good heart." We are still friends to this day. I was genuinely happy living on Love Beach, one of the most beautiful I had ever seen with its small coves, its powdery white beaches and tall trees. Lyford Cay market was only four miles away, and I was free as a bird to do what I wanted when I wanted. I had plenty of friendly neighbors from all over the globe, and my friend Valerie had made enough introductions so I didn't miss out on any social events.

David was a forceful, self-confident man and capable of dealing with me. He was comfortable with my independent lifestyle and I was comfortable with our long distance relationship. His main base of operation was San Francisco, and he also had a home in Carmel, California, where he lived with his family.

Occasionally he would fly out to see me, though the Bahamas were not his idea of a place to relax. He preferred the south of France and other places around the globe. However, he knew I was happy and safe in the Bahamas, so he put very few demands on me. Since he took such good care of me, I believe it was one of the happiest times in my life.

I joined the Lutheran church in Nassau. Once a week, I would make the effort to be sober on Wednesday evenings so I could attend Bible study. But in the whole year I lived there, I probably didn't make it to Bible study more than half a dozen times. I just couldn't keep from drinking. Once I started to drink, I lost count of the drinks and of the time, until I couldn't remember much of anything. Although I continued to drink, I don't remember being lonely, except for occasionally missing David's companionship. I stayed busy with food shopping, preparing meals, sitting on the beach in the morning, talking and getting to know on a superficial level my neighbors, who were quite an assortment of characters. I loved to hear their different accents and the stories about where they were from and what had brought them to Love Beach. I was fascinated when I was sober enough to be coherent.

I tried not to go out in public when I was too bombed. I was afraid I would make a spectacle of myself like my mother had done when we were living in the Washington, D.C. Nary Yard. I think David realized there was no point in trying to communicate with me after noon so I didn't expect him to call after that time. I was good at casual conversation, and although I tried, I had no idea how to bond with people. There were so many times when no one could reason with me, so I was extremely difficult company. Since I would drink in the afternoons and into the evening, I spent the major part of my time there alone.

Nineteen-eighty-four was the year I discovered hard liquor as the source of my comfort, rather than wine. It didn't seem to matter if it was Scotch, vodka, gin, or rum. Each was as powerful as the other. In the Bahamas, Liquor was cheaper than milk, a British imperial quart only cost about six dollars. Liquor took the sting out of life. It made the deep-down loneliness in my soul bearable; it was the only way I could understand life or cope with it. Life became more and more acceptable with the quantity of liquor I consumed.

A series of men were interested in me and drifted in and out of my life. I didn't take anyone seriously except David. It was comforting to have occasional human contact, but I didn't want to become involved. I just couldn't handle it and I didn't want to try my luck again. David kept his distance psychologically, and that was something I needed at that time in my life.

In December 1984, I met Gabrielle, who was from Switzerland. We clicked and are still friends. She was quite outspoken and opinionated, which turned off some people, but I thought she was just plain terrific! She was very wealthy, quite cultured and intelligent, and didn't seem to need anyone else. We enjoyed each other's company, even though her idea of a drink was a thimble of sherry. I couldn't believe it when I saw her nurse a tiny glass of something for HOURS! I finally had to bring my own drink with me when I visited with her.

At Christmas she introduced me to her friend, Norbert, who was from Bavaria. He and I spoke the same language when it came to alcohol. We spent New Year's Eve together and we bought a case of champagne magnums to celebrate. If one were enough, then twelve would be better! He was the first man to make a big deal about my sailboat. He thought I was remarkable, and I thought he was terrific for thinking that way about me. I think I fell in love with him because he was one of the few men in my life who believed in me. I didn't know how to believe in myself; I had lost confidence in my ability to dream and to set goals, probably after Brent lost interest in me. Whatever the reason, my dreams were vague, but Norbert was an architect and a master of building from dreams to reality. Suddenly I wanted to sail my boat and decided to make that my goal. I wrote to the Chapman School of Seamanship in Stuart, Florida, and signed up to take a class to become a sea captain the following summer. After Norbert left we tried writing and calling each other, but eventually we faded out of each other's lives.

Occasionally, I met David in New York or San Francisco. We stayed at the futz in New York, but he rarely could persuade me to leave the hotel room. He tried to lure me out for shopping or earing, but I was usually content with room service. David would read, work or watch the news, and I would watch him or look out the window at Central Park. I loved looking at the beautiful trees. I don't remember what occupied my mind and my thoughts other than the beauty I observed, which included David, who was lovely to look at. He had a strong Nordic face, topped by a magnificent crop of dark blonde hair, brilliant blue eyes and strong, even white teeth, which sparkled when he offered me his very sexy smile. I wish I had drawn his portrait.

During those years, my life was pointless and wasteful, but I didn't know what to do to rectify it. I was a beautiful woman, but that was of no value to me with my emotional pain. David tried and tried to reach me but to no avail. I just couldn't be reached. I am sure that dealing with me was extremely difficult for him.

David told me I would drink until I was crying hysterically, then I would pass out, but I don't remember my behavior. When I was sober, magical things would happen when I dared go outside. One day in San Francisco, as I walked to a hair appointment, I saw thousands of colorful balloons filling up the sky. It was the day the cable cars were reactivated, and I was privileged to see all this magic. It was as if the sky were filled with colorful polka dots!

David caught me by surprise one Saturday in San Francisco when I wasn't drunk. He took me out on a day so clear that the blue in the sky was brilliantly vibrant. 'We drove to Mill Valley and then into the countryside to an adorable English Tudor restaurant where the food was authentically British. It was the first time he asked me if I really "had to have that drink." His question took me back briefly to the first moment I met him in Barcelona in November 1969 when he was in the US Nary. I felt a sense of magic right then and I really DID need to "have that drink." It was as if I was determined never to feel happy. David often said I seemed determined to self-destruct. I needed to hurt myself to prevent my getting close with anyone. It was the only way I knew how to operate.

Walking with David along Central Park during a snowstorm one day, I studied his profile amidst the snowflakes. His collar was pulled up, and in that split second, it dawned on me that I might love him. I felt overwhelming terror because I was sober and vulnerable. I thought he would hurt me if I let myself love him, and that pain would be too intense for me to survive. I couldn't get to a drink fast enough! At that time I seemed to be losing my grip on reality and my sanity.

In April 1985, the lease on my little apartment in the Bahamas was up. Since I'd signed up for the Chapman School of Seamanship in Stuart, Florida, I decided to go as soon as possible and not wait for the summer class. I was determined to learn how to navigate and to become a sea captain. David tried everything in his power to discourage me; he felt things were just fine the way that they were. David was rapidly becoming exasperated with me, but an alcoholic on a mission can't be told anything!

My boat had been docked at Lyford Cay in the Bahamas for a year, and I sailed from there to Nassau. I had it hauled out for a bottom job, provisioned it, and moved onboard. I called the Chapman School of Seamanship and had them send me some men for a crew. I thought they would be competent sailors since they were from the school. My destination was the Manatee Pocket in Florida, home of the Chapman School.

After the three men arrived, we sailed via the Northwest Providence Channel, setting a course for Port St. Lucie. In the dark of night, I was on watch alone. My crew was down below asleep and I didn't have enough self-confidence to order them to help me. Lights appeared out of nowhere, and I thought it might be a city. I frantically checked my chart but couldn't figure out where the light was coming from. I understood that I was off course and that I must be near Freeport. No one had told me there were no tall buildings in Freeport. At the last frantic minute, I looked hard and long through my binoculars and realized that the lights were the rear of a huge freighter. She had lost all power forward and I was headed straight for her! There was some fancy dancing to be done, and rather quickly! I did some maneuvering, changing my course drastically. We didn't hit the freighter, but the maneuver woke up one of my sleeping crewmembers. I asked him to sit with me for the duration of my watch. At that point my instincts told me that none of these men had ever been on a sailboat in their lives, but I didn't want to accept the fact that none of them had a clue about how to sail. I dismissed my feelings since I couldn't take the truth, not then! I had been told the men had been in the Nary and were good students at Chapman, but I was discovering they had had no practical experience in sailing. I felt like I was with the Three Stooges.

The weather got worse, the wind picked up and began to howl. The seas began to churn and water gushed over the bow. Finally, I saw the glow that meant we were approaching the Florida coast, but just then the engine quit. My VHF (very high frequency) radio began to lose power. My guts were right. None of these men had the slightest idea what to do. I guess I could have tried to put the sails up, but I was afraid of the speed the boat would gain in the high winds. It was chaos and I was so scared that I might have to pee, I didn't drink any water, much less alcohol. I had just enough power in my VHF to call the Coast Guard for help. They had me count down from ten over and over again until my battery died. The Coast Guard found us in the middle of the raging sea, and one of their sailors managed to jump aboard my boat and fasten a bridle for a tow. The Coast Guard towed us into the Palm Beach customs dock and helped us tie up. It had been a long and frightening night, and at five o'clock in the morning, I collapsed in my bunk.

I was awakened a couple of hours later by a commotion on the dock; the authorities were knocking on the hull. I came above and asked what they wanted. Apparently one of my trusty crewmates had scaled the fence to go for a pack of cigarettes. He was a wanted felon, and to make matters worse, he was now in custody for having entered the country illegally. I was so worried about my engine and about getting on with the voyage that I don't remember how I managed to avoid being responsible for him, but I do remember he was taken away.

I tried to find someone to help me discover what was wrong with my engine, but there was no time. I was holding up space at the customs dock and I was asked to leave as soon as possible. Instead of fixing the engine, I located a boat willing to tow me to the Manatee Pocket, which is a few hours north of Palm Beach by boat. As if I needed more grief, we ran aground in the Pocket, which is usually very shallow, and the DEA (Drug Enforcement Agency) boarded my boat looking for drugs. Penelope, my cat, chased the drug dog off the boat. I had to remain in the Pocket for some time because of low tide. The water wasn't deep enough for my boat, and I had to wait for high tide to come in. It had been an exhausting and hair-raising adventure!

School soon started and I was doing well in most of the subjects, with the exception of learning about engines. They were not my forte. Navigation, weather and boat handling came easily to me though, so I thought I was in the right setting.

David called and asked me to meet him at a hotel at the Palm Beach airport. When I met him there, he told me I had totally lost it. He couldn't take my behavior anymore and said I was now on my own financially. When I told him of my plans to become a sea captain that spring, he told me that I was *definitely* on my own.

I was in a manic state at the time, so I had no idea of the real consequences of my behavior. Manic-depression in an alcoholic can be deceiving. One can think it is the alcohol making the person act irrationally, but in reality the insanity is already there. I gave David the impression that he wasn't needed. In reality I needed his protection and his financial assistance. However, in my manic state I lost my grip on reality. Since I needed money, I flew back to Nassau and sold the car I had brought over from Florida in 1984.

Chapman School had a hands-on class, which entailed physical work and the actual maintenance of a boat. While painting the bottom of one of the school's boats, I lost my balance and landed in some paint. I realized then that I was in the wrong place at the wrong time. If I should be painting anything, it should be my own boat! As I wound down from my manic state, I began thinking more clearly. I marched into the office and asked them how I could go about getting my second semester tuition refunded since I was just at the end of the first term. They explained that I needed to quit right then, so I did. I quit as impulsively as I had begun.

I didn't understand that once off a manic state, I could think a bit straighter, but not for long without medication. All I knew was that I had suddenly changed the course of my life drastically and I was not in a place to make any more drastic decisions. All I wanted was to go home, which at this point was my boat. I had to take it somewhere I felt safe and I decided to sail to Fort Lauderdale. Since i felt I knew nothing about sailing, I called a friend in Fort Lauderdale who was a boat captain. For a reasonable sum of money, he agreed to come up to the Manatee and assist me.

It was the Fourth of July, 1985. I was so disappointed that I didn't have an interest in pursuing a career as a boat captain. All I could think was that I hadn't followed through on something I had started, and these thoughts were the beginning of a deep depression.

I found a safe dock in a good section of Fort Lauderdale on Hendrick's Isle, one of the two islands in the downtown section set aside for people who want to live aboard their boats. My boat had two iceboxes and no navigation station, so I hired a carpenter to tear out the icebox that was oversized and build a navigation desk and seat in its place. I designed the freezer to be under the seat. Renovation meant there would be tools, lumber, sawdust and total chaos for awhile on the boat. While the renovation was going on, I rented a furnished apartment in the complex where my boat was docked.

During this time, I was experiencing shakes and serious hangovers, but I was also seeing a psychiatrist. He insisted I go into the hospital to dry out for a few weeks, and I agreed. A psychiatrist visited me at least once a day in the psychiatric unit and encouraged me to try Alcoholics Anonymous. I couldn't think why I would need their help. I didn't know of anyone in the AA program. Certainly i could handle my drinking problem on my own! After all, both my parents had tried AA and it did not work out for them. I didn't know what AA entailed and the institution of Alcoholics Anonymous scared me.

It was the first time I had been in a hospital where I was assigned a social worker. She told me I wasn't in touch with my feelings. I wondered what "feelings" had to do with anything. Obviously there was a connection between my feelings and my emotions, but what? I just didn't want to be dependent on booze anymore. But I couldn't deal with sobriety. The only feeling I was in touch with at this point was anger. I had no idea that "anger" could be an issue. It was one emotion I should have and could have worked on while in a hospital setting. I wasn't ready, nor was I capable, to deal with my emotions. The idea of feeling anything emotionally made me fearful.

Somehow, I acquired some marijuana. Since I was given passes to leave the hospital, I would go out to my car and get stoned and just sit there. I had been diagnosed as an "alcoholic with reactive depression" who also had a "personality disorder." I hadn't been diagnosed with bipolar disorder at this point. Smoking the grass helped me dismiss my problems and my aimless life.

Unfortunately for me, the hospital released me. I was on my own to figure out what to do next. The hospital couldn't do anything with me until I was "ready" to listen to reason and make an effort at recovery for myself. I needed mental help desperately, but I didn't know what that entailed at that time. I was in denial of my dependency on chemical substances, which I felt helped me with my psychological disorder. I was very hardheaded, blind and really sick and I didn't receive the help I needed. I wasn't ready to work on myself I was alone and I was a mess.

12

Despair and Illness

I had two girlfriends who were sisters; I had known them since 1977. I felt a great deal of warmth from them, but it was their loving, kind and very patient mother whom I was drawn to the most. They invited me to attend their church, which was Baptist, and I wanted to go. I had converted to the Lutheran faith in 1982, but I was also drawn to the fundamentalism of the Baptist Church.

I knew very little then about the Bible, and I wanted to learn more. It was not easy to know what to believe or which church to follow. Due to my marriage annulment, I was too angry with Roman Catholicism to even consider attending the Catholic Church again. During my Catholic high school days, I had been reprimanded for being an independent thinker. The Catholic Church, my father and the nuns had drummed into my head that I needed to follow. It seemed that I had "followed" all my life as a result of this training. I had taken orders from my father, from the nuns and from Eastern Airlines for forty years.

I decided to attend both the Baptist and the Lutheran churches because that is what I wanted to do. I enjoyed the familiar ritual of the Lutheran faith, and I also enjoyed the Bible instruction and music in the Baptist church. The only complaint I had about the Baptist church at that time was that little time was spent in silence. Because of my Roman Catholic upbringing, I valued spending quiet time reflecting on my life, my failings and the praise and worship of God. The loud conversations, the clapping, and the jovial attitude felt inappropriate in the House of God. I wasn't accustomed to the different atmosphere, but I took what I could from both the Baptists and the Lutherans.

During this time I visited David again in New York. He still seemed to care about me, and he was the only person I was sexually intimate with. I tried staying sober, but I felt like I was going to lose my mind and whirl the window in a state of anxiety. I couldn't handle this level of anxiety so I got stoned on marijuana. I had not had a drink since I went into the hospital. I had never handled anything of importance as a sober person in my life! David hadn't been around me before when I smoked dope. He didn't complain; he just said I tasted "smoky" when he kissed me. We were once again at the Ritz, overlooking Central Park. I was too stoned to go anywhere, however, I was still anxious. I didn't know where to go or why I had these feelings, but they were so real and terrifying.

David had always been patient, generous and tender. He was now the best thing in my life, but I couldn't accept it. He only expected me to want to be intimate with him and give him a kind word or a smile or possibly a "thank you" for some of his kindness. However, being around him made me want to scream and crush my feelings. Now, many years later, I realize that I loved him. But there was no way I could admit that to him or to myself. I wasn't sure of David's feelings for me. I couldn't imagine how he could love me after observing what a nut case I was. Since I had a low opinion of myself at that time, I felt in my heart that he would reject me or hate me, so one day I simply vanished.

I went back to Florida, to my boat. I got the boat situated in the Bahia Mar Marina in Fort Lauderdale and provisioned it for a six-month cruise. Mike, the man from Chapman's who had helped me bring my boat down to Fort Lauderdale, agreed to go on the trip. His stipulation was that I didn't drink. I hired a boat captain for the crossing.

In late November 1985, we headed for Nassau, Bahamas, via the Northwest Providence Channel. Just east of Great Harbour Cay my bobstay broke. The loud bang sounded like a gun being fired and really scared me! The bobstay is the part of the structure that holds the top of the mast to the hull of the boat.

When my shipmates checked the damage, they also discovered that the line from the jib had dropped into the water and caught on the propeller. Since the engine was running, the line was so snared and tangled that the propeller was stuck tightly. Now we couldn't start the engine either! I had spent much hard- to-come-by cash for the captain's salary, and he could not help us. We were floating in the middle of absolutely nowhere, with no engine and no jib. We bobbed around and the sun sank in the sky. I couldn't stand one more minute as I watched the sunset. I felt so let down and frustrated I went below, found a bottle of Courvoisier, and poured myself a drink. After four months without a drink, it didn't take long before I finished the bottle and passed out. I don't know what I would have done if I hadn't had that bottle-probably had a nervous breakdown. I was very disappointed in myself for having gotten drunk. It depressed me because no one else seemed to need it as badly as I did. I wish I had seen that I needed help for my drinking problem before I set off on this journey.

We managed to make our way into Nassau Harbor seventy-two hours later, exhausted because we had to sail with only the mainsail and it was tedious. The harbor was full of commotion and we were in the way of landing seaplanes. We dropped anchor somewhere near Club Med. The loud noise from their band didn't even bother us. We were miserably tired and fell asleep as soon as we hit the bunks.

The boat captain returned to Florida and somehow Mike and I got the boat to Brown's boat yard, where the boat got fixed-many dollars later. I decided, once again, to hire a captain to get us to the Caribbean. The only captain I could afford was Davey Jones. Yes, that was his "real" name, and he brought lots of bad luck with him. When Davey arrived, Mike left. Mike couldn't stand my behavior when I drank. Davey turned out to be an alcoholic, so I had someone to get bombed with every night.

We arrived in Staniel Cay in the Exuma chain of the Bahamas just in time for Christmas. Christmas morning I discovered there was no dinghy attached to the boat. I asked Davey where he had put it. "Well," he claimed, "there was a dinghy there last night, as far as I can remember." I couldn't blame him because I could barely remember the day or night before myself.

Losing the dinghy with the outboard motor was an extremely expensive experience. Not only did we not have transportation to shore, but I had to replace the dinghy and buy a new outboard motor. During the docking at the Staniel Cay Yacht Club, the propeller shaft backed out of the coupling. This part of the engine is quite important because it is part of the propulsion system. Davey somehow rigged the boat so we could get down to Georgetown in the Exumas.

At that point, I felt my boat was being held together with chewing Bum, Popsicle sticks, and rubber bands! As we brought the boat in under sail to the dock, we were under control and gallantly gliding by all the boats at anchor. It was cocktail hour and all eyes were upon us. Davey left me at the wheel and went below for something. I headed straight for a sea wall! I couldn't help it! Suddenly Davey came back up and changed our course 180 degrees—we were just inches from disaster! We sailed back past all the boats and people, who by now knew we didn't have a clue how to dock under sail. It was the height of the season and the harbor was quite full. I hated the idea of smashing my boat up as that evening's entertainment! Somehow we managed to get docked with the help of the people on the dock.

Davey flew back to Fort Lauderdale to get the shaft fixed and to replace the dinghy and outboard motor. I was there at the dock alone with my car, Penelope. Since it was January, it was too cold for swimming or wandering around. I had time to finally relax and enjoy my boat with no one else on board for the first time since I owned it. I lightened up on my drinking and felt very serene and content with my life.

A few weeks later, I flew into Fort Lauderdale to buy more provisions, to pay for the shaft, the new dinghy, and an outboard motor. I needed to charter a plane to get all of the stuff to Georgetown, and it was a huge expense. Money was going out and none was coming in. I decided to go to the Royal Bank of Canada in Nassau to take out the last amount of money I had left to my name.

'When I returned to Georgetown with the needed items, Mike, my former shipmate, who had left because of my drinking, decided to rejoin us. A man named Scott wanted to come along on the cruise and Davey returned as well. That made four of us to take the boat the rest of the way to the Caribbean. Early one Sunday morning I discovered my old cat, Penelope, was missing. On Monday Mike and Scott went to the elementary school in Georgetown and asked the children to help them find Penelope. One of the children found her dead on the beach-apparently she'd fallen off the dock, drowned and washed up on shore.

In all my life, I had never bonded as deeply with anyone or anything as I had with this cat. She seemed to love me unconditionally and never hurt or disappointed me. She was the closest thing I had to having a child; she had been everything to me for sixteen years.

If I had been unbalanced prior to this, I really flipped after Penelope's death. I was too numb to drink, but in my insanity I grabbed my mini-fourteen semiautomatic rifle and my dead cat, climbed atop the laundry facility, adjacent to the marina, and was ready to die. My crew managed to talk me down without any harm being done. They put me on a plane and arranged for me to go into the psychiatric unit at Holy Cross Hospital in Fort Lauderdale. This time there was a new doctor assigned to me. He suggested the possibility that I had a bipolar disorder, which would require medication. Finally, someone realized my need for serious medical help. The doctor prescribed lithium for me.

While I was in the psychiatric unit, I felt like I was in a helpful haven. All the nurses were trained in psychiatry. One nurse in particular took a deep interest in my case. "Joni, bipolar illness, which is also referred to as manic-depressive illness, is not something to be ashamed oi" this kind nurse told me sympathetically. "You need to be aware of your manic states and your depressive states and you have to be responsible for taking your medication. There's no cure for this disorder, but many people have this disease."

"I'm relieved there's a label that goes along with my madness. I used to think I was totally out of my mind," I told her. I had bonded with her, appreciating her understanding and gentleness. I felt so safe at this hospital.

"Thank God it's a treatable disease. I know you're thankful for that. But you've got to have a doctor to carefully monitor the medication," the nurse emphasized.

I had never monitored my different swings of highs and lows. But very slowly, ever).thing made so much more sense to me. I thought it would make my life easier now that I understood that when I felt wild, it was nothing more than a manic state and I could ride it out.

Just before my fortieth birthday in 1986, my friend Ruby came to take me out of the hospital. She flew with me to St. Maarten. My boat, the *O Nauti Jonni,* had left the Exumas, where Penelope had died, and had arrived in St. Maarten on March 23. When the crew discovered I was out of money after paying them for delivering the boat, they left.

I was on my own. I sailed to Oyster Pond on St. Maarten and docked at Captain Oliver's Marina and Restaurant. Fortunately, I still had my American Express Card and my monthly disability check. I rented a car, since Oyster Pond is quite a distance from Phillipsburg, the main town on the Dutch side of the island. At that time, there was nothing built around the restaurant and the marina. I had to go into Phillipsburg daily for provisions and my mail.

One day I spotted a lad with curly golden hair hitchhiking. He was carrying a tool kit and since he looked a bit "salty" I prayed to God that he might know something about boats. It would be a good thing if I met someone who really knew what he was doing. I picked up Henry and we hit it off the moment we met. His intelligent green eyes danced with mischief and he looked about my age. He told me he was in his thirties and was a British citizen. I was very attracted by his intelligence and his cultured manner. Most important, he was very witty and, yes, a bit "salty." He made me laugh! We became inseparable friends, and I later discovered he was about ten years younger than he had originally told me.

He had lost his passport, so we few up to Nassau to the British Embassy and remedied the situation. He was given another passport and all was well. He had made a commitment to deliver a boat to the Panama Canals Pacific Ocean entrance. Originally he would have taken the boat to Australia, but Henry now decided to go only as far as Panama because he wanted to return from Panama and marry me. That was an unexpected surprise! There was just something so real about Henry. David was serious and dedicated to making money and didn't do giddy things like Henry did. I was so attracted to Henry because he was a good-natured man and a joy to be with at all times.

"Joni, I want to give you my uncle's signet ring. It's my only valued possession, but I want you to keep it."

"Are you sure?" I asked him. I was very surprised at his touching gesture.

"It's a promise from me to you. I'm going to come back after I take the boat through the Canal."

I was smitten with Henry and touched that he would give me his precious ring, which was all he had to give me. I knew he was serious and my feelings were verified when he kept in touch by letter and with expensive phone calls.

I went to Miami to see what I could do about Eastern Airlines. They wanted to fire me because they doubted I was really sick enough to remain on disability. I had been put on disability in 1983 after my hysterectomy because I had had a nervous breakdown and I fell into a deep depression. Back in 1983, the psychiatrist then deemed me unfit to continue my job as a flight attendant. Eastern wanted to have psychiatric testing done on me to determine if I was actually unable to remain as a flight attendant.

The union representative put everything she had into my case. She said the union would do its best to preserve my job, as I was entitled to remain on disability for five years before a judgment could be made regarding my job status. At that time I had been on disability for three years, and a psychiatrist had since diagnosed me with manic-depressive disorder. Eastern asked me to go through a great deal of testing and I cooperated. Their doctor said, "You are either lying, or you are indeed very sick." He had never seen someone quite so delusional. How does one explain alcoholism interwoven with bipolar madness? I certainly couldn't!

That summer while I was in Miami and Henry was in Panama, I stayed at the apartment of an Eastern Airlines pilot named Wally. I had known him since 1978 when we had both been based at Kennedy Airport in New York. We had been distant friends for all these years. Now I needed his friendship more than ever, and more importantly, I needed his hospitality. The Miami apartment was his "crash pad." He lived in Denver with his wife, but he was based in Miami and flew from there. The apartment was located in Kendall, just south of Miami International Airport. I was the patient/friend who came to sleep on his sofa for one night and never left. We became close friends as the days became weeks and then months. I had to remain in Miami until Eastern Airlines had all the information they thought necessary about my condition before they could make a decision. Wally was rarely there since he was either in Denver or working a trip.

I was renting a car by the week. I took part-time jobs with temporary employment agencies to pay for the car, food, phone bills, gasoline and my vodka. My life at this point was totally unmanageable. My broken boat was sitting at a dock in St. Maarten, Henry was in the Panama Canal, and I was sleeping on Wally's sofa in Miami.

One day in November, Henry called. He was finished with his boat delivery in the Panama Canal and needed help with getting my boat from

St. Maarten to St. Thomas. 'Wally few down to the islands to help him. Henry and Wally delivered the boat to St. Thomas and then returned together to Miami.

Since we were all together, Henry and I decided to have our wedding with Wally as the best man. We were married in December 1986 by my dear friend, Pastor Jim. Pastor Jim had coached me in the Lutheran faith back in 1982. Henry and I had a small private service with only our friends Claire, David and Wally. Now both Henry and I were sleeping on Wally's sofa. Henry started the procedure at immigration to get his green card so he could start working legally in the United States.

One night, for no apparent reason, Henry and I bought a female puppy. For Wally it was the straw that broke the camel's back! "I can't believe the two of you. You don't have a place to live, Henry doesn't have a green card, and Joni doesn't know what's happening with Eastern, and then you go get a dog. That's totally insane!" Wally fumed at us. "That's it! You're going to have to leave my place, right now"

We moved in with my old boat captain, Davey Jones. Since his live-in girlfriend was an alcoholic, there was not a sober moment. We were one huge, drunk, dysfunctional family! In those days, I kept a diary. Now, when I try to read about how life was for me, I become queasy trying to grasp how I was able to survive. My life was like a roaring fire to which more and more gasoline was being added.

For some reason that I don't remember, Eastern Airlines gave Henry and me passes to fly down to St. Thomas in May of 1987. As if things were nor crazy enough already, we bought a baby ferret and named her Lucretia. 'We brought her along with us as well as our puppy, Emmy Lou.

I was devastated when I saw my boat. It was barely floating and had been robbed of almost everything. Books were ruined because hatches had been left open and rain had fallen into the boat. It was literally a floating shell. I couldn't blame anyone, as I was in Miami when all of this had taken place. Henry did the best he could to find work in St. Thomas and cope with our battered boat. There wasn't much work available in the Virgin Islands since there were a great many people looking for jobs in the marine field. I was blessed; I had a monthly disability check coming in that paid for our food.

One day I had one of my "awareness checks," and it dawned on me that life didn't have to be this awful. I asked a friend, who was a veterinary technician, if she could take my beloved ferret, Lucretia, she was overjoyed because they had become fast friends. She was so excited she bought another ferret to keep Lucretia company. The only reason I can explain this sudden state of rational thinking is that I was out of a depressive state and starting to go up into a manic state. The state in-between the manic and the depression gave me tons of energy and much clearer thinking.

I asked Henry to call a crew placement service in Fort Lauderdale and ask for a job, and to please take the first job offered to him. Henry got a job quickly and few up to Florida.

Slowly, I began to figure out what to do about the wreckage of my life. I decided to let my boat remain in dry dock in St. Thomas since I had no money to remove it anyway. I flew back to Fort Lauderdale with our dog and tons of luggage. However, it was such a short-lived coherent state and I was getting confused again. By the time I was back in the States, all I could do was put one foot forward and hope the other would follow.

Fortunately, when I arrived in Fort Lauderdale, Henry met my fight with a rental car. He was working aboard the motor yacht *Janette,* whose owner was notorious for being cheap, but we thought that was okay as the job provided good benefits. The job gave us a sense of security we had not known before. Henry had received training as an engineer aboard a Shell tanker, and he was adapting well to the job as engineer on this motor yacht.

He had to remain on the yacht for long periods of time, so I needed a place of my own. I went to see my friend Jude, who was looking for a roommate. It was summer, and she let me bring my dog. I slept on the back porch. My credit was still good and I was able to buy a car. Henry paid the insurance and my car payments. He and the motor yacht were in New Jersey that summer, and somehow I made it through that time on Jude's back porch. She had a small back yard, so my dog actually had her freedom and her own domain.

In the fall, though, I needed to move on and find another place to stay. I visited my friend Leslie, who had become a well-established movie set designer. She was working on the film Winter People in North Carolina and suggested I house sit for her family home in Nashville, when I contacted Leslie's mother, much to my surprise, she was delighted to have me house sit.

Leslie's mother was in Alcoholics Anonymous. She was the one who planted the seed about AA, but she didn't try to educate me. She had simply said, "You will know when you are ready." It was just what I needed to hear at the time. I tried to control my drinking by only drinking wine, and not the first thing in the morning. I didn't want Leslie's mother to think I was an out-of-control alcoholic!

I stayed in Nashville until Thanksgiving. During that time, it never occurred to me that I was lonely. It never dawned on me that I needed other people in my life. I was very much alone with my little dog, Emmy. Henry called me in the middle of November to tell me the boat he was working on would be in Fort Lauderdale soon. It was getting cold and rainy in Nashville. The timing was right for me to leave because the family was arranging for some relatives to move into the house.

Henry had booked a hotel room and Emmy and I arrived in Fort Lauderdale the night before Thanksgiving. On Thanksgiving Day I was deeply depressed so Henry and I started drinking together, and we both got very drunk. We got into an argument in the parking lot of the motel where we were staying and Henry backhanded me. He claimed I had hit him first. This was the first time I had been hit by a man, and the reality of it was too much for me. I fell down on the pavement crying and screaming. I went totally out of my mind!

The police came and tried to remedy this mess. They claimed I was suicidal and took me to a crisis center at the general hospital, which was very crowded. Thanksgiving must have been the day much of Fort Lauderdale went mad that year. The general hospital kept me for seventy-two hours, then sent me to a private psychiatric hospital. I remained there for three weeks.

Henry came to visit me every night. One night he was sitting on my bed when the doctor came in. He listened to both Henry and me relate to each other and when Henry leaned against my bed and started to cqr, the doctor suggested we both get therapy. Looking back, I wish we had. Perhaps it would have helped Henry with his lack of responsibility and a lot of pain and bad feelings might have been avoided. Henry was funny and charming but would retreat within when the situation turned serious. I knew after his crying episode that he needed help and couldn't be the strong person I needed to lean on.

During the last few days in the Fort Lauderdale hospital, I developed foot drop, which is the inability to lift the foot. This condition was tied to my back injury in 1979, when I was injured in flight during Hurricane David. I was transferred to Holy Cross Hospital where the doctor, who was an orthopedic surgeon and a friend of mine, said I had a seriously herniated disc. I was put into traction.

"You must make a decision about which type of surgeon you want to perform the surgery," the doctor told me. "The difference between my specialty and a neurologist is like the difference between a football player and a ballerina, and you need the expert."

Needless to say, I opted for the neurologist. When the neurologist came to see me, I saw he had a peacefulness about him, and I knew the surgery would be all right. I asked my beloved Pastor Jim to administer communion the night before the operation. He suggested I also ask for a private duty nurse because this would be a serious ordeal and he was worried about my care.

'When I regained consciousness after the operation, both Henry and the private duty nurse were there. Everything was all right until the spasms came, then I panicked! I was scared to death already, and I just couldn't take much more. The nurse gave me a shot of Valium and finally, after a long battle, I slept. I was really touched that first night. I awoke several times and Henry was right there sitting next to me. In spite of our marriage, I had never really considered that he loved me. I never dared to ask him; however, right then I felt as close to being loved as I had felt when Brent had loved me-a long time ago.

After I was released from the hospital, our friends Terry and Merle asked if we would house sit for them and take care of their Siamese cat, Champers, while they were in England for several weeks. It was another one of those unbelievable coincidences again, when I was being provided for despite myself. During this time, Henry borrowed enough money from the owner of Janette to have my boat delivered to Fort Lauderdale from St. Thomas. I put the boat in dry storage since I didn't have the ability to get on and off of it by myself so soon after surgery.

'When my friend Merle returned from England, she put her foot down about my drinking. She asked me not to drink in her home. It was the beginning of summer, and Henry's yacht was going to New Jersey for the summer season. I called my pilot friend, 'Wally, who was now living in Sparta, New Jersey, and asked him if my dog and I could come for the summer. It was fine with him, since he had gotten over his anger with Henry and me, so off we went to New Jersey to be near Henry.

I try not to be too quick to decide if someone is an alcoholic. Over time, I've learned that someone may appear to be an alcoholic because he or she just drinks heavily; however, in essence, they can stop at will. I hesitate to say if Wally was an alcoholic. We certainly drank alike, as far as I can recall. Every day I would start the day off with a beer, and we would offer one to the mailman when he appeared before noon. I was not fond of beer, so I would switch to wine after the one beer and drink wine until 4 p.m. Wally and I would go out for happy hour daily. Then I would drink hard liquor and slip into oblivion.

One evening while we were out drinking, I became ill. Wally suggested I drink only soda or anything without alcohol. That was successful for awhile, but then I'd order a drink and get sick again. On the way home, I had to stop the car several times to heave. I noticed that I was throwing up blood. I was truly in denial; I was trying to ignore it! That night I couldn't sleep because of the pain in my stomach. It was unlike anything I had ever experienced. In the morning I called Linda, a close friend. She was a registered nurse and I trusted her. She very calmly told me to go to the emergency room immediately and explain my symptoms. I asked Wally to drive me to the hospital.

All I remember is telling the nurse how I felt. The next thing I knew an I.V. was put in me, I was put through a cat scan, and then I was sent to the intensive care unit. My pancreas was hemorrhaging and they discovered I had pancreatitis. As they were putting the tube through my nose and into my stomach, I thought it would really have been a lot easier to let up on my drinking instead of creating all of this fuss. I cried when they were inserting the I.V into my chest. I felt terribly sorry for myself and defeated. All I wanted to do was drink and be left alone, but it wasn't working out that way for me. Some of the emotion I felt was the release of my feeling that I had to fight the world alone. It was over. I had lost my battle. The hot tears streaming down my face were the last thing I remember as I slipped into a coma. I stayed in the coma for three weeks.

While I was in the hospital Henry was in Mexico working aboard the motor yacht *Magnifico* based out of Berkeley, California. Henry kept in touch by phone with Wally, who gave him updates of my condition.

One night my old friend Linda, the registered nurse who had been my first real friend and my roommate at St. Mary's school, came to my bedside. "I just want to tell you I love you, Joni. I'm here for you," Linda said softly. "I'm so glad you took my advice and got to the hospital."

I shook my head and mumbled. I couldn't focus and I couldn't speak. I did, however, feel a bond that was stronger than steel and as pure as the finest gold. I wanted for nothing; I was at peace. When I think back to that moment, I realize I felt very willing to die and just be done with this life. But someone or something was pushing me to live.

When I got better, Linda told me she had driven five hours from Washington, D.C., to be with me because the prognosis wasn't good. When she located Wally to ask him how to find the hospital, he wanted to know if she would join him for a drink. She told me she was furious with him and had no use for him after that.

One day I came fully out of the coma and asked the nurse if I could have something to eat. She went to the nurse's station and all the nurses came in with tears of joy in their eyes. They circled my bed and welcomed me back. I felt embarrassed and very weak. The doctor ordered me Jello. I told him I wanted something heartier, like a pizza! I was anxious to get rid of the central I.V. because it was making me itch like crazy. I bounced back to the land of the living. My recovery was pointed out to me as a "miracle." I concluded that maybe I had more to accomplish in this lifetime after all. I didn't feel special, and I didn't have much awareness of spirituality then.

When I arrived home from the hospital, Wally was acting oddly. He opened a can of beer and let the spray hit me. "I'll bet you're sorry that you can't have one," he declared, and I knew it was time to leave. I called Henry and he flew into Newark, New Jersey, to help me drive my car to Berkeley, California, where he was stationed onboard the motor yacht, *Magnifico.*

13

Trying to Recover

When I was strong enough to travel, Henry and I drove to Berkeley. It felt like the longest road trip I'd ever been on in my life. I thought we'd never get out of Nebraska, but we made it in less than a week to California. The owner of the yacht had a ranch outside of Berkeley. The ranch house on the property was the crew's quarters where the staff and their guests could rest and relax. Finally, my little dog Emmy had a whole ranch on which to play!

I didn't take a drink then, even though there were a lot of parties. I was trying with all my heart to keep from taking a drink because the doctor had told me the pancreatitis would reappear if I did drink. However, I didn't have a sense of finality about my drinking yet. I had almost died, but neither I nor anyone else was that concerned about my drinking.

When Henry went back to work on the yacht, I headed up the highway to Eureka, California. I saw a turnoff for the Parducci wine factory and decided to stop because Parducci was my favorite wine. It is difficult to explain why I would do this, but I just *had* to buy a case. I didn't intend to drink it, I thought. I just bought it and put it in the trunk of my car and continued on my journey. At that time I could not see the total insanity of this action. I was still in complete denial that I was an alcoholic and that I had almost died from this disease rather recently.

When I arrived in Eureka, I located the College of the Redwoods, where I intended to study art while Henry was on the yacht. I was fortunate to rent a room in a tiny, humble home in Fortuna, California, which only cost me one hundred dollars a month.

My landlady's name was Beth, and she played a very important role in my life. Beth was a Seventh Day Adventist and determined to keep the Sabbath(which for her was Saturday) as holy as possible. This meant preparing the Sabbath meal in advance and not allowing the washer or dryer to be operated on Saturdays. She had the most "Christian" attitude I'd ever observed in my life because she literally lived what she believed. Beth was different from anyone I knew; she was non-.judgmental, for one thing. This woman was grateful for everything she had, and she taught me the art of having "an attitude of gratitude!" When she was growing up in Oregon, her family had dirt floors. Now that she had linoleum floors, she was so grateful because they were easy to keep clean. I was amazed that someone could actually be grateful for their floors!

Beth explained to me that God was a very caring Father and that He had always given her exactly what she needed. Some of the things He had given her were lessons, she said, and the hardest thing for her was learning the necessary lessons so she could move on in life. She was a vegetarian and asked me to refrain from cooking meat in her home. She had never eaten meat and didn't like the smell of it. I watched her closely and was intrigued by her deep dedication to her faith and her love for God. She definitely left an impression on me about what was involved in being a Christian.

I worked very hard on my class work and my art homework. My hard work paid off and I received excellent grades. My life was going very smoothly until the day I thought about having a drink. Thinking that one glass of wine a day would be a nice way to spend an hour, I went to a lounge in Ferndale and ordered a glass of wine. I had one glass of wine that day, but eventually it was two, and then it was the case of wine I bought at the Parducci Winery weeks before. I didn't stop there. Soon I was buying a liter of wine a night and consuming it.

Henry came up to visit as often as he could. He didn't seem concerned that I had resumed my drinking. My artwork wasn't suffering, but I was going to school with terrible hangovers and headaches and slowly losing my drive and energy. I had to drop algebra, because I had to be able to think, and I was not blessed with the mentality to drink and concentrate on math at the same time.

I thought by changing my location I might not need to drink. This is very common misconception for the alcoholic mind. I think I was also in a manic phase, which makes people do impulsive things. Despite Beth's companionship and her warm little house, I wanted to be in a more active location. I transferred from the Eureka campus down to the Mendocino branch of the College of the Redwoods so I could be near the ocean. For the alcoholic, there is always the delusion of a "geographical" cure!

I was very fortunate to find a tiny cottage to rent across the street from the Mendocino Center of Art and Museum. The interior was very sweet and decorated with Laura Ashley wallpaper and accessories. There was even a fireplace. I was living in a perfect location to be happy, but I found I was still lonely.

My pal, Leslie, had suggested I go to Adult Children of Alcoholics. ACOA is a huge organization and the meetings last for one hour. I decided to see what it was all about because it sounded like something I could relate to. Since they had tapes and books to loan our, I borrowed some tapes and heard people testify how happy they were in recovery. I heard laughter and the mention of gratitude. Through ACOA, the door to sobriety seemed more and more possible and appealing.

At the Adult Children of Alcoholics forum, feelings were discussed and my inability to deal with any emotions became a real problem for me. I had trouble bonding with people as well, so I didn't make friends either. Life was bearable only after several drinks. It was difficult to try not to get too bombed for the meetings. I didn't want to be drunk, yet I couldn't stand the emotional pain I experienced when I was sober.

When I was drinking, there was a point where I would either maintain a high or pass out. I never knew what my limit was. There was such a fine line for me between being high and passing out. I would appear normal even though I had had a considerable amount to drink, and then BANG-I was out like a light.

I sought out a psychiatrist to help me with my feelings of despair and the feelings of elation I had soon after the depressions. I found a doctor who had retired from the staff of San Quentin Prison in San Rafael, where he had worked for many years. After listening to my history, he told me there was no doubt I had bipolar disorder. He recommended a medication that would treat me for depression, anxiety and panic disorders. I took it and it worked! The manic states didn't get out of control to the extent that I was irrational and my panic disorders dissipated almost entirely. This medication was called Triavil. This doctor, who was very pro-ACOA, also brought to my attention that I needed human contact. I needed someone to talk to and to share some time with.

———————

In the fall of 1988, Eastern Airlines asked me to fly to Miami to sign all of my retirement paperwork. I was to be considered retired in September 1988, with major medical, a pension and fight benefits for life with Eastern. I did this and returned to Mendocino to continue my art class.

One day the boatyard in Florida where I kept my boat called. They told me the yard had been sold and wanted to know if I wanted to keep my boat. New management was going to auction off all the boats in dry storage in ten days. Of course I wanted to keep my boat and I didn't have much time to waste!

I had to quit my art class, which shattered me. I feared this was my last chance at art school. However, my boar was really my home and I had to save it. I was not happy about having to leave. I felt angry, confused and frustrated! Instead of fighting to stay with my art and figuring out this situation with my psychiatrist, I drank. I packed the car and headed for Florida with Emmy Lou, my pooch. Henry was in the Caribbean at this point. It was difficult to keep track of him during this time because of the distance involved. I got to Florida in time to claim my boat. I had kept in touch with my pilot friend, Wally, who had left New Jersey and was living in Florida again. He helped me paint the bottom of the boat before I put her back in the water. Henry showed up for a couple of days, and they both helped get the boat ready, out of the boatyard, and into my old dock on Hendrick's Isle.

I was back in Florida again, living on my boat and drinking. That summer it rained and rained and rained and my boat leaked. It was a pretty miserable situation. And I just kept drinking, only now it was vodka instead of wine. In August of 1989, my pancreatic symptoms returned.

I was terribly unhappy and just knew I couldn't continue feeling this emotionally miserable. I called a psychiatrist who had once been my doctor at Coral Ridge Psychiatric Hospital in Fort Lauderdale. He was hesitant to admit me to the psychiatric hospital because of my pancreatic history and the fact that my pancreas was flaring up again. He suggested that I go to the emergency room.

At this moment I made the conscious decision to get sober, regardless of my physical condition. I decided that if I was going to die, I was going to die SOBER! Finally, it seemed that I had the will to discontinue drinking alcohol —what Leslie's mother had told me about. "You will know when you are ready," she had said. I never thought to go to an AA meeting. I couldn't go many hours without shaking, sweating and heaving. When someone was as addicted as I was, it was a painful process to withdraw from the substance of abuse.

I went to see my friend Carolyn one afternoon. She said I looked as if I was going to die. Not only did I feel death creeping up on me, I *looked* it! I came back to my boat after visiting Carolyn and fell on the hardwood floors sobbing. "God, please help me," I begged.

Suddenly, I felt like someone was cradling me saying, "There, there, it's going to be all right." I felt a sense of release and an awareness that I needed to call the doctor and get myself admitted to the treatment center as soon as possible. And I did. I was admitted to Coral Ridge Psychiatric Hospital that night.

The first night I was in the hospital, just before I fell asleep, I sobbed and sobbed tears of relief that I was ending this way of life. I had not a clue of what to expect, but I was willing to give whatever the doctors suggested a chance. I wanted to think clearly and function without using alcohol. Many nights I walked the hall thinking that surely I would die because I couldn't sleep. I had no peace, only constant anxiety. One day led into the next day. It was too early in my sobriety to understand "one day at a time." Right then, I was living one minute at a time-second by second! Eventually I was taking afternoon naps and sleeping the whole night through. I felt bright as a box of birds, but I still had trouble with the shakes. I shook for the three weeks I was in the hospital.

One night, very early in the AA program, I was in the TV lounge and noticed a tall, lanky blonde woman smoking a cigarette. She seemed to have everything under control. If smoking works for her, I thought, then there is a chance it can help me as well. You could say that I was just trading one addiction for another. Maybe so, but it wasn't mind-altering, and it gave me something to focus on besides myself. The woman's name was Irene and we became inseparable pals. She was the friend and the contact I needed. She had a wonderful sense of humor and made the three weeks in the hospital actually enjoyable. When we left the treatment center, I started to realize how my Higher Power was looking out for me. Because of Irene's impending divorce, she needed me as much as I needed her. We were both without our mates. She did not have a car and I did. We did everything together and I did the driving. We stuck together like glue for our first ninety days of sobriety.

14

One Day at a Time

When I got out of treatment, I started to see how God had a plan for my life. All I was required to do was check in with Him daily, ask for His daily guidance and thank Him at the end of the day if I was sober. "Please don't form any expectations and you won't be disappointed," was what I heard from my prayers. It was a simple beginning and one I could cope with at that time.

I would pick up Irene, my AA buddy, early in the day and we would do our errands, eat our meals together, and try to plan our day around an Alcoholics Anonymous meeting. It was exactly what I needed. I needed to learn the fundamentals of living a sober life. Just walking, talking and driving as a sober person was new for me. We managed to go to the suggested ninety meetings in ninety days. After not drinking for ninety days, as a sign of our accomplishment of continuous sobriety we each received a red poker chip. I think the color choice has to do with the importance and significance of those first, most difficult, ninety days. Poker is symbolic of gambling and the chip is a reminder that we are gambling with our lives. I could remember the times when I was consumed with when I could take my first drink of the day and how I could stay drunk. To be without a drink for ninety days was an awesome accomplishment I didn't even try to comprehend it. I just lived exactly as they suggested-ONE DAY AT A TIME.

Henry arrived in Fort Lauderdale just after I completed my ninety days of sobriety. He was astounded at the change in me. I had the boat organized; I was coherent and a pleasure to be with. He asked me what he could do to assure my sobriety and because we had very little money, I told him to please get a local job. Since it was the Christmas holiday season and work was readily available, he got a job as a sales clerk in a department store.

All we could afford that Christmas was a poinsettia to decorate the interior of the boat. We went to Christmas Eve services at the Lutheran church. My dear Pastor Jim had grape juice set aside to give me when we took communion that night. At that Christmas service I knew a much stronger force than me was in control of my life, and I surrendered to Him and let Him get me through one day at a time. My expectations were in check. It felt as though I had stepped into another dimension. This all came about because I let it happen. I did not get in the way of this Force. AA had suggested that I try this, and it appeared to be working for me.

In Alcoholics Anonymous, women stick with the women, and the men stick together to work what we refer to as our "program." I was told I needed to find a sponsor. A sponsor is a confidante to turn to in time of need. A sponsor, a man or woman, should be everything that one wants to be like in respect to being sober. My first sponsors name was Susan. When I went into treatment I thought for sure I would be so glum and boring that no one would ever find me funny or interesting again. I really feared I would never laugh again. Susan told me her story with such humor that I had to hold my sides because she was so honestly funny! I called Susan at times when I was so confused it was embarrassing. I took the chance that she might make a fool out of me or chastise me, or even reject me. But she never did any of those things because she had walked in my moccasins.

Through the program of Alcoholics Anonymous, we change and as we change we have different needs. Eventually I changed sponsors. My next sponsor was Elynore O. The first thing she did was take me to dinner and then to a meeting. The usual format is to go to a meeting and then go for coffee and conversation after the meeting. Elynore wanted to discuss any problems I might have beforehand and instill in me an element of expectation for the meeting. She had been sober for over thirty years and had even managed her own alcoholic treatment center in Montana.

The first assignment she gave me was to write my life story. I wrote everything about myself in only eleven pages! I submitted it to her, and she circled everything she felt I needed to expand on in red ink. It was dripping with red ink. She wanted me to write my story in longhand to get the feel of writing out my emotions. I wanted to type it, so I did. We butted heads on several subjects, but we remained "sponsor" and "sponsor." Despite it all, I had a great deal of respect for her, and I even grew to love her. It had been a long time since I could trust my heart to open. She told me, "Take baby steps. One at a time."

Elynore had totally devoted her life to AA. She had been a successful career woman with more than three careers. She had also had a family, raised two sons, and buried one of them. I found her to be remarkable in her energy level and stamina, right up until her death. I'm sorry I continually insisted on my way then. If I had yielded to her wishes, she would have been able to teach me so much more, and I could have been farther along in my AA recovery program so much sooner. I would have been a much wiser woman. Elynore, as my sponsor, tried to save me a lot of pain and time.

Trusting another person was one of the most difficult things I had to learn as a sober woman in the first years of my program. I had never been able to trust any-one-EVER! It had never occurred to me to let go of my will and to let go of my fear. I had never known any other way but My own way! I had to please men during my past life, yet I got my own way in the end. Now I realize just how bullheaded I was. I had to literally learn how to live, think and be. Elynore was there for me and willing to take me by the hand and walk with me through a new way of life-one day at a time. She taught me to say the Serenity Prayer and to lean on that prayer and use it as often as necessary.

The prayer is:

God, grant me the serenity to accept the things I cannot change, The courage to change the things I can And the wisdom to know the difference, Living one day at a time, enjoying one moment at a time, Accepting hardships as a pathway to peace, Taking this sinful world as it is, not as I would hate it, Trusting that You will make all things right if I surrender to Your will, So that I may be reasonably happy in this life and supremely happy with You forever in the next, Amen.

15

Sobriety

The months led into a year of sobriety. There had been times when I felt the impossibility of having a week of sobriety, and now I had a whole year! And I had done this for myself and no one else. It felt like a huge accomplishment. I had to be selfish on this issue; it was my life. If this was possible, then I could do anything! I got stronger and braver by the day. Henry was so proud of me that he helped me sell my sailboat, which entailed a lot of work for him. With that done, we moved into an apartment, and I was able to get my things out of storage. These were belongings I had put away when I sold my condominium in 1984. Opening boxes in 1989 was a treat because I had forgotten what I owned and stored away!

This time was my first opportunity to "play house" as a sober woman. There were responsibilities I hadn't realized when I had been married before while drinking. I loved the role I played as a wife. I put my whole heart into it and it was very rewarding. I enjoyed not having to work for a living and having the opportunity to leisurely plan the evening meal. I enjoyed the food shopping and the usual things one does on a not-too-busy day.

Henry obtained a job as an engineer aboard a boat in Miami, which came with a good salary. I took the money I got from selling my boat and paid off his debts, bought him a car, and paid off my car. I was still in debt for almost thirty thousand. But I wanted to help Henry, who was young and had acquired debts of his own, get a fresh start. I had had my turn, and now it was his turn for a chance at making it.

I was advised go to Consumer Credit Counseling Service to consolidate my debts and get a grip on what I owed; however, the odds were against me. I found out that six months after I got out of the treatment center, there had been a mistake in my Eastern Airlines records. I was informed I did not have any medical insurance and was told to pay the treatment center ten thousand dollars. I was shocked to get this news, but I decided that somehow I could handle it. After all, I was stronger than I had ever been in my life. We worked out a payment plan. I would just be paying them off for the rest of my life! But things got worse. When I had retired from Eastern Airlines, I had not reported this fact to CIGNA, my long-term disability insurance, which had forfeited my right to CIGNA disability insurance altogether. CIGNA wanted a check for eight thousand dollars "immediately." I presented this whole dilemma to Consumer Credit Counseling Service, and they suggested I file for bankruptcy since I didn't have an alternative. This was such a humiliating reality. I had once had so much, and now I was trying to scrape together enough money just to pay the attorney to go to court and rectify this mess.

In spite of the pressure I was under, I didn't take a drink. The thought never crossed my mind, and I found that pretty amazing. A drink would lead me to a "drunk' and that would just confuse the issue. It took me months of payments to the attorney to get to the bankruptcy court, but it got done. The main lesson I learned was that I didn't need to drink over this situation.

Now I literally had to learn from the beginning how to be conscientious with money. I cannot stress how difficult this is for someone who suffers from a manic-depressive bipolar disorder. During the manic state, I would feel a high, almost as if I had taken a large quantity of cocaine or coffee. I would manifest a feeling of great wealth and spend money irrationally and recklessly. The worst thing for me was using a credit card and being unable to anticipate the consequences of saying, "Charge this, please." I can't emphasize how impossible it was for me to think there wasn't enough money SOMEWHERE.

A manic state hit me around November 1990. I didn't know at that time what some of the danger signals were. First, I couldn't sleep, and then the grandiose and irrational ideas began to appear. I went to a department store and applied for a job as a buyer. I was given the job, a credit card, and a considerable discount. By five that evening I had bought seven pairs of shoes (some that didn't fit), an expensive watch for Henry, clothes for both of us, and had maxed out the card!

A person with my manic-depressive disorder cannot safely walk into a shop with cash or a credit card during a manic state without buying something. There is a definite "high" that accompanies the spending of money in a manic phase. However, once I'm down off the high and it is over, it is incomprehensible to me how it happened in the first place. It is something like a blackout, and I am left with the bills, wondering what to do about them. At least there were lots of gifts for Henry under the tree at Christmas in 1990!

Once again, we went to our midnight Christmas Eve service at the Lutheran church. My pastor was so proud of me. I had come a long, long way from where I was when I was studying to become a Lutheran in 1982. He had seen me trying to cope with life, and he had great hopes for Henry and me when he married us in December of 1986. Here I was in 1990-happily married, safe, and sober. I was a sight for sore eyes!

Henry was being trained to become an assistant minister at our church. His father was a retired Anglican minister living in England. I was very pleased when Henry informed me he aspired to follow in his fathers footsteps and become a minister as well. We started to make plans for Henry's new career. He would have to apply to a Lutheran seminary in the United States. We both agreed on Pacific Lutheran Theological Seminary in Berkeley, California. Fortunately for both of us, we were now more secure financially and there was no reason why we could not go forward with the application for admission and a request for a government loan. 'We took it one day at a time.

With the boat sold, the complications of life were reduced. We both got stronger and braver for this new adventure. I had one stipulation that Henry didn't agree with, I wanted him to live in the dormitory for the first year of his seminary training. I felt he needed the structure. It had become very obvious to me that Henry was indeed fifteen years younger than me, not only in years, but emotionally, too. He had some serious growing up to do.

During this period our marriage began to change. I was working with the Alcoholics Anonymous program, and I was growing and changing. I had to focus on myself because I had much to learn about life and lessons to learn about myself. I felt Henry needed to do the same thing with his own life, the reason I suggested he live in the dormitory. I felt he had much more growing to do that didn't include me. Unfortunately, as I grew, it became more and more obvious just how little we had in common. Henry stopped speaking to me and then withdrew totally from me. He made the decision to buy a station wagon to tow my car to California. He started to make decisions that didn't seem rational to me.

I fell into a deep depression and had to enter Coral Ridge Psychiatric Hospital. While I was there, the counselors presented a serious reality to me when they asked me what I planned to do about my depression when I got to California. What would I do when I didn't have my Fort Lauderdale support system? In spite of their advice, I became more and more unrealistic. I thought everything would be fine. I wasn't worried about taking a drink because, after all, AA was a worldwide organization, and I had some contacts in California through some friends. I could only visualize the best. I wanted to live back in Mendocino, where I had been so happy with my art and had discovered Adult Children of Alcoholics. Now that I was sober, I could not imagine why the whole picture appeared so bleak to everyone else. I had a true Pollyanna approach and no one could seem to get through to me.

Unfortunately, I thought that as a wife I had no say and no choice but to follow my husband to California. So, in August 1991, Henry, my dog Emmy, my new cat and I drove across the country to California. I had gotten my cat, a little black female, as a kitten and I called her Sobriety Cat because she had been born on the day I collected my red poker chip that signified I had been sober for ninety days. 'We towed my car behind the station wagon. We were so loaded down with boxes that the only place for Emmy Lou to sit was in the litter box! It took us about a week to get to California. In all that time, Henry didn't speak a word to me. Henry had not been very communicative since I had gotten sober. It was evident he was angry.

Having lived in Mendocino in 1988, I knew the area and was able to find accommodations. I rented a house trailer behind a feed store way out in the middle of a redwood forest. I could afford it because it was only three hundred dollars for the rent and fifty dollars for the heat. Henry dropped me, my car, the animals, and our boxes off at the trailer with a sense of vengeance I had not seen in him before. After everything was unloaded, he headed for Berkeley and the "Holy Hill."

The next time I saw Henry, I knew instinctively that the marriage was over. He didn't have to say anything-I could see it in his eyes and I could feel the negative vibrations. It hurt terribly. I felt like it was all my fault because I had insisted on keeping my animals and I knew that unless we could rent a house in Berkeley, I would have to part with them. There was no way we could afford a house near the seminary on our budget. All along I had felt certain Henry would snap out of this glum angry state until I saw him that day. I knew then that he was even more bullheaded than I was. We had been through a lot together, but I could tell that none of that even fazed him. He was finished with me.

There I was in a trailer behind a feed store in a redwood forest in Northern California, alone with my cat and dog. At that time, I didn't know anyone else in the area except my neighbor, the landlady. She was a very serious Jehovah's Witness and had no use for me, except for my three hundred and fifty dollars a month rent. She tried to convert me and when that didn't happen, I had the feeling I was either despised or just tolerated.

I refer to this time of my life as my "desert experience." I felt as if I were alone in a desert, having to fend for myself both emotionally and physically. I had never been this alone before in sobriety. I decided it had to be a test of some kind from my Higher Power. I had to believe in something to justify the mess I had gotten myself into this time! This had been exactly what the staff at the psychiatric hospital had warned me about while I had my bout with depression just a few months back in Fort Lauderdale. I had plenty of time and space in which to think things out this time. I needed to have a plan, so I sat in my bedroom on the bed looking out the window, smoking cigarette after cigarette. My landlady had asked me not to smoke in the trailer. I had agreed not to smoke before I moved in; however, I had not planned on being marooned behind the "redwood curtain" either!

I think everyone needs a desert experience to discover one's priorities. My experience was helpful in simplifying my life and also gave me the direction I needed. It helped me clarify, what was important and to move on with my life. I knew my Higher Power must have had a reason for everything that was happening. I just had to roll with the punches. I knew I wouldn't get very far just sitting, so I went to the local hospital and volunteered to help out wherever they needed assistance. There, I realized I had nursing potential. I worked at an information booth one dal', and on another day pushed a cart around to all the hospital rooms with beverages and snacks for the patients. I liked working with the sick and the elderly; it came naturally to me. I loved being needed and being of service to these people.

Winter came and it was cold, foggy, and desolate. All I had coming in was my disability check and my small pension from Eastern Airlines. I had no money for a hot cappuccino in one of the cute, cozy coffee houses, no view of the crashing Pacific surf, no fire in a fireplace, no large, comfortable chair to curl up in-this was stark reality! The only view I had was an uprooted field where I watched my cat try to catch scurrying rodents. I was alone with myself and slowly I lapsed into a deep depression. It was very difficult to pull myself together enough to get to the hospital to do the small chores required of the volunteers, but I put one foot in front of the other and managed to at least look good, despite my depression.

I returned to see the psychiatrist in Mendocino who had originally put me on Triavil in 1988. From what I told him, he was convinced that Henry was having an affair and wanted me to look into it. I didn't really care what Henry might or might not be up to. I just wanted him to grow up and face some of his issues and deal with them. If he couldn't find it in himself to grow and change, then I didn't want him in my life. Henry no longer had his sense of humor. He had turned into an angry, disagreeable and selfish man. He had just had the station wagon repossessed and was overwhelmed, I am sure. If anything, I knew that Henry was scared.

He had lost his mother when he was ten years old and that kind of scar is difficult to heal. I wanted him to get well, but I also wanted him to put some effort into his own healing. Surviving and maintaining my sobriety were my two main concerns. The only insecurity I recognized for myself then was economic insecurity. As a woman and as a person, I felt strong and secure. I didn't know where Henry stood on his issues because he wasn't talking to me after his car was repossessed. I was very lonely but long-distance calls to family and friends were out of the question. My income didn't allow for it. The redwoods and the solitude made it more evident that I was very much alone in my struggle to survive.

While volunteering at the hospital twice a week, I met Maddy, who was the head nurse on the evening shift. She was also in the AA program, and we slowly became friends. I invited Maddy over to my trailer twice for a meal and she was impressed with my cooking. Some people had approached her at the hospital about needing a nurse to take care of their father, who was an Alzheimer's patient. When they asked her if she knew of a nurse who would be able to cook and care for him, she called to ask me if I was interested. I needed the work, and I told her I d be very interested. I interviewed for the job and was hired. It took some time to get to know the patient. Clarence was an eighty-four-year-old widower who was in the early stages of the disease. I knew very little about Alzheimer's, so I read everything I could get my hands on, especially the *Physicians Desk Reference* and the *Merck Manual.* As I read, I realized he and I were both disabled in our own ways and maybe we could help one another.

Once he realized I wasn't out to interfere with his life and that I was there to be a courteous friend, we became good pals. I enjoyed cooking for him, and he loved my cooking. I baked apple pies until he was popping out of his shirts and his family grew concerned! I started to leave off the dollop of vanilla ice cream and started using milk in the mashed potatoes instead of cream. We shopped together and did our errands together. He was so appreciative when I took him for a ride along the sea. Some nights we would park on the bluff and watch the sunset, when he was lucid, Clarence would get tears in his eyes. He would look deep into my eyes and say, "Getting old is really hell." I understood him. I suppose it was because I remember what my grandparents went through. I could also relate to his condition because I was disabled with manic- depression, which is no picnic either.

Every morning Clarence would get up before dawn, dress and go outside to spend the entire day digging ditches for fences. Every night his son would come with his bulldozer and fill up the holes. Clarence was getting exercise daily, even when it rained.

One day, out of the blue, my old friend Wally, the pilot, appeared. He had been my friend through thick and thin. He only stayed one night because my landlady screeched at him that his big sheepdog could not stay on her property. He offered to loan me the money to get my furniture out of storage in Florida. He also offered me a room, rent free, in his home on the West Coast of Florida. I didn't jump at the offer because I felt some responsibility for Clarence.

Things changed when Henry, informed me he wanted a divorce. I felt ready to move on with my life and circumstances have a peculiar way of happening for the best. Frank, the man I had lived with in New York City in 1975, called me. He asked me if I would consider moving to New Jersey to take care of his mother. She had fallen and fractured a bone in her hip, and he desperately needed someone to live with her in her home, which was a couple of hours from Manhattan.

During these past nine months, I had watched my life being shaped by a force much stronger than myself. I choose to call that Divine force My Higher Power. All this time, I had never been without food, gas for my car, food for my animals, nor nice clothes to wear. I had everything I needed. Learning the art of patience was a very important lesson for me. Suddenly I felt very special because during my "desert experience," I could tell that I was growing up. I had judged people all my life until I got sober, and I was now learning to have compassion. I was being released from having to judge other people. I knew I had always been a poor judge of character anyway, so releasing this compulsive urge became a wonderful relief. The moment I had this realization, I thought I heard a voice telling me, "First walk a mile in their moccasins before you judge them."

By the spring of 1992, Clarence had developed an advanced case of prostate cancer and the prognosis was nor good. He was getting much worse and needed live-in care, which I could not provide. I decided to take Frank up on his offer to help his mother in New Jersey. He wired me five hundred dollars to help me get on the road. I had all my things in California packed up and shipped to 'Wally's house in Sarasota, because that was where all of my other furniture was by then. I had the trailer professionally cleaned, so I could leave it in good order and remain on good terms with my demanding landlady.

When I was ready, I set off down the coast through the redwoods and then headed east across the country with my dog and cat. It was Emmy Lout fourth time to cross the States by auto. She looked up at me with her wise brown eyes as if to say, "Well, Mom, here we go again." And off we went! I didn't turn on the radio because I knew this journey had lessons in it for me. I was open to suggestions from my Higher Power, as I knew so little about the universe and life itself. Most importantly, I was willing to try to absorb whatever this Force wanted me to know. Somehow. I knew I needed to work on my pride. I had heard people say that one is not humble if one admits it. Pride is such a natural instinct and one thing I didn't want to part with. Me and my big ego. I knew something had to give here. Pride is the first of the seven deadly sins.

In the middle of the desert, somewhere in Utah, I felt in my purse for my wallet to get a gas card. I couldn't locate my wallet! It had been quite a while since I had filled my tank. I became quite anxious, searched frantically everywhere, and thought I had probably left it where I last stopped for fuel. My heart sank as I realized I had probably left it hundreds of miles back. Fortunately, I had some cash stored elsewhere in the car, so I stopped for gas and called Frank in New York. I asked him to call about my gas cards and to please have them all cancelled. I no longer had any major credit cards, but in my wallet I did have all of my personal identification and all those things that signified who I was. I drove for a while and then realized just how vulnerable I really was as a woman alone.

I was hurt because my British "Prince Charming" was no longer in my life. My circumstances were all too much for me right then. I started to cry. Sometimes it takes just one little thing to set us off and cause us to finally sense our feelings. Something was penetrating through layers and layers of superfluous, negative programming. I started to sob, and I realized just how badly I needed to forgive Henry. He had used me to get his green card and to get on with his life. I had used him to get out of my situation in the Caribbean and he had supported me through the first eighteen months of my sobriety.

Fortunately, there was no traffic on the highway. There were beautiful billowing clouds in the sky and only salt flats around me as I drove through Utah. I could feel the presence of God, and I sobbed until I was drained. I had surrendered. I gave up my will and my always wanting my own way I let go. I asked God to guide me through what remained of my life. I had been drinking in 1976 when I met Franks mother sixteen years ago. I couldn't remember her house or her, and now I was headed for New

Jersey to be her nurse. I marveled at how life just keeps on going, despite our efforts to get in the way and complicate things. Life just has a wall, of its own. I no longer felt in charge of my life, and it felt very good to me after forty-six years. I was comfortable knowing God was in charge of me and of the universe. When it was time for me to exit for fuel I decided to empty my trash bag. I took the bag out of the car and on top of the trash was my wallet!

It took me eight days to drive to New Jersey. Frank's mother was the personification of the patient from Hell, a control freak! No one I knew was so determined to control life, people, and the outcome of every circumstance. This situation was more difficult for me because Eastern Airlines had trained me to control people as part of my job as flight attendant. Controlling others was something I had to work at all during my flying career. In spite of this training and experience, I was absolutely bewildered about how to deal with this woman, who was immobilized by a fractured hip. I could help her with her physical limitations, but when she would lift the receiver and listen to my private phone conversations, I began to wonder why she was so invasive.

I had never handled someone like her, so I decided it was time for an AA meeting. I called the fellowship and a man and woman picked me up for a meeting. I was grateful to them because at the meeting I realized just how close to picking up a drink I had been on that day. My nerves were frayed. I had to develop some coping skills for this care-giving position, and attending the meetings helped me. I felt better knowing how to safeguard my sobriety' Once Frank's mother accepted me, we adjusted to each other and things went very well. She wasn't that terrible after all. Even Emmy Lou enjoyed going in to visit her in her room now and then. Much to my amazement, she tolerated and enjoyed my dog!

When Frank's mother developed a bleeding ulcer, she had to be admitted into the hospital. Her health continued to fail, and the family informed me I wasn't needed anymore since she would be entering a nursing home.

16

More Challenges

When the job in New Jersey was over, I left for Florida with Emmy Lou by my side and Sobriety Cat in her kennel. From New Jersey through the southern states was another long journey. It gave me plenty of time to mourn the loss of my marriage and my husband, Henry. I had to come to grips with the fact I would never see him again. But I was also relieved because I could not see myself as a minister's wife. I didn't feel I could have taken on all the responsibility required for such a role.

It was a relief to see Wally in Florida, waiting in his driveway for me. I was in for a rude awakening. He had gone to a psychiatrist and had been diagnosed with having panic attacks. He had been promoted to captain, but he could not pass the landing tests in the simulator due to these attacks. He, like myself, had received early retirement disability from Eastern Airlines, I had thought I was coming to a safe haven but I soon discovered I had been lured into another difficult situation, a continuation of isolation and loneliness.

Wally declared half of the house was his private domain and that I was not to cross over into his territory. This was not so terrible, but he even divided the living room! I was expected to provide the food and prepare his meals, but I think he also expected me to take over the role of housekeeper. I had trouble adapting to this very weird experience and whatever role he had in mind for me. He was adamant that ours was to be a platonic relationship, and he ignored and rarely spoke to me after I moved into the house. It was evident he wanted a maid and I was it. I felt isolated because I still found it very difficult to make friends. I had to get on with my life, so I went to the local hospital and signed up to do volunteer work in the emergency room twice a week. I tried to stay busy during the day and stay out of the house.

Wally started accusing me of being a doormat because I didn't report Henry to immigration for using me to get his green card and also for his wanting to divorce me. Wally was an angry man, but I hadn't seen that side of him before. He thought I should do my best to get even with Henry and to try my hardest to have him deported. Wally was big on revenge and became verbally abusive. There was a reason for the bitterness he was taking out on me. Wally had just gone through an ugly divorce and had lost half his retirement to his ex-wife. He was particularly angry because she had cheated on him the entire time he had been flying.

I'd never been trapped in a house with this kind of behavior before. I was very confused and I needed help. I was able to locate a therapist who accepted Medicare. She became my confidante and offered me solace during this troublesome time. Moving out would be difficult because Wally claimed I owed him two thousand dollars for saving my furniture and shipping my things from California to Florida. What had been a good friendship dissipated into a bare minimum of tolerance. It was a tumultuous summer, besides Wally's antagonism, there was Hurricane Andrew to deal with.

While working at the hospital that year, I met a pulmonary surgeon who invited me out for lunch one day. John was interested in dating me, but there was one catch. He thought I was co-dependent and needed some serious counseling. Even though he had this superior attitude about me, I was fascinated with him. Formerly a Jesuit priest, John had left the priesthood for medical school and when he graduated had converted to Judaism. He had his vulnerable side-he hated being bald and wore a toupee. Once I saw him without his toupee, but rather than let me see him bald, he put a washcloth on his head! He looked pretty silly!

Since we both agreed I had this disorder, I consented to go into Charter Glades Psychiatric Hospital as an inpatient for their ten-day program. Four other patients and I were admitted for the ten-day program in a private wing of the hospital. Our first assignment was to pick out a teddy bear at a mall. I found a stuffed pink pig I named Piggy Bear. The program included a great deal of intensive therapy, both one-on-one and group. In spite of this, I didn't feel as if I was becoming any wiser about myself or anyone else. The program seemed to be an expensive attempt at treating lifestyles that had taken us a *lifetime* to develop. The doctor dropped out of my life after I was released from the hospital. I wondered later if he had a financial affiliation with the hospital. As it worked out, my Medicare insurance paid for the ten days of inpatient treatment.

I went into a manic phase in November 1992. My life was going absolutely nowhere, but I had clarity and energy. I needed two thousand dollars to repay Wally and get on with my life. I decided to try to find work, but there was nothing that interested me in Sarasota. I contacted a friend in Fort Lauderdale to find out what was available there. My friend suggested I draw up a resume and submit it to a crew placement service for work as a stewardess aboard a luxury motor yacht. I got my resume in order and submitted it to several of the yacht and crew placement services in Fort Lauderdale, which is the yachting capital of the world. I had no idea what the job entailed; it just sounded like something I might be able to do.

Much to my surprise, I got hired on a hundred-and-ten-foot private luxury yacht based out of Turnberry Isles in North Miami. The salary was good. They were anxious to leave for the Caribbean immediately because they were behind schedule. I knew the boat would be gone for at least six months, so I hurried back to Sarasota and got my life in order. I told Wally I would eventually be able to pay him the money I owed if I took this job. Instead of being overjoyed that he would be reimbursed, Wally was angry I would be leaving. As his neighbor, Janette, had pointed out to me before, he had enjoyed verbally and emotionally abusing me for all these months.

I reported aboard the yacht within the week. I was issued a different uniform for every duty: I had an outfit for tending the bar, one for working during the day, and one for serving the meals and working in the evenings. I was called the "heads and beds stewardess." Most of my jobs were behind the scenes, which was okay with me since I was breaking into a new field of work. It took some time for me to realize that the routine was dreadful. I was up at 7 a.m. to help set up the buffet breakfast. While the guests and owners ate, I went below to the staterooms, made the beds, collected the wet and soiled towels, and took the towels below to the washer and dryer. I then dried and buffed the marble showers, tubs and floors. I had to make sure the glass, mirrors, chrome, and toilets all sparkled. And that was just the morning schedule!

I spent the afternoon doing laundry interspersed with shining and buffing various things onboard. While the evening meal was served and eaten, I repeated the morning routine-only in reverse: the beds needed to be turned down, chocolates placed on the pillows, and Perrier water placed in the ice buckets between each bed. There were ten guests, the owners and six crewmembers. Since there were only two washers and two small dryers, I was usually up until two or three in the morning doing laundry.

The schedule became too much for me. I had come aboard on November 16, but I didn't last until Christmas. The captain took me aside and confided that he was afraid I might have a heart attack or collapse from fatigue if I kept up the pace. I don't know how the routine went for the other people who came before me, but I chalked it all up to just being too old to keep up with the chores. Also, my manic phase was winding down and I could feel my energy dissipating, not to mention my enthusiasm.

When we arrived in St. Thomas, the captain gave me an airline ticket so I could return to Florida. I flew back to Miami defeated. Wally met my flight. In the car, Wally handed me a joint of marijuana. All I could think of as he handed it to me was that it would relieve some of the emotional pain, exhaustion, and humiliation I felt. The reality of my life at that point was too unbearable. It was not the best time for me to fight for my sobriety. I honestly felt that the best thing for me at that very moment was to flow with the way Wally wanted things to be.

When we arrived at his home, I was in for a complete shock. The living room furniture was totally rearranged, and there was a new sofa to replace his treasured row of actual airline seats he had used for living room seating. Wally said my bedroom was now occupied, as well as the guestroom, and I would have to sleep in his bed. It was very late and I was too exhausted to argue. I was depressed and stoned from the grass and I felt beaten.

Very early the next morning there was some commotion in the living room and I went out to investigate. The neighbors, Janette and her two daughters, were occupying my room and the guestroom. The children were getting breakfast before going to school and the TV was blasting away. The two young girls were talking over the television, and their mother was yelling at them. These people had been evicted from their house shortly after I had left for the Caribbean, and Wally had permitted them to move into my room. He had taken most of my personal effects and stuffed them into a closet. It was a terrible shock when I saw the condition of what had been my room and my things.

I felt totally invaded and I reacted hysterically. Once again I was unable to cope with my life, and I was admitted to the Psychiatric Crisis Center. It was a Friday and there was no doctor on duty to make a diagnosis or to prescribe medication for me. I had not taken any of my medication with me when I had left to work on the yacht. As a bipolar patient, I needed to take my prescribed medication, but it is so typical of a patient to avoid medication before a manic. The "high" feeling is contagious and unbelievably pleasurable. The hospital staff didn't know what to do with me except to let me ride out my manic state.

I was a raving confused maniac. I needed to get some rest, which was difficult under those conditions. A manic phase rarely lets a patient sleep. I had needed a safe haven and to be sedated, but I didn't find either of those things in the crisis center that weekend. While I was there, Wally brought me my Christmas mail, and I was surprised to receive a Christmas card from my first husband. I called to thank him for the card, explaining the bind I was in with no money and nowhere to live because Wally had thrown me out of his house. Brent was then a successful doctor in Huntington Beach, south of Los Angeles. "You are no longer my responsibility," he told me.

I was disappointed to be so flatly rejected since I had invested time and money in him during our marriage. I had never asked him for anything until this phone call. Then I remembered why I had never asked him for anything before now. He had always been stingy, mean and selfish to me. Why did I expect him to react differently this time?

When I was discharged from the hospital seventy-two hours later, Wally picked me up and took me to a rundown motel o, the seamier side of town. I was jobless and homeless and my only company was Sobriety car. Before I'd taken the yacht job, I had given my dog away to an animal-loving couple in Ft. Lauderdale. I couldn't afford to stay in a motel—cheap or otherwise. I was alone and scared. I realized then I had burned too many bridges. There was absolutely no one willing to help me. I needed to get on my feet and on with my life. I tried playing, and the only answer that came to me was, "God helps those who help themselves." I took that to heart and rve.t job hunting. I found work aboard a yacht in Palm Beach. That job only lasted a week. I was caught by the owner's wife while sampling the smoked salmon off an hors d'oeuvre tray. I felt like Oliver Twist because I had never been fired for eating before! I was really desperate.

The only thing I could think to do was to call an escort service for a job. I wasn't thinking about adultery, greed, or lust—just survival. I reached a woman by phone who asked me for my driver's license number and told me she would return the call the next day. I couldn't imagine why she would want my driver's license number. The next day she called to tell me to pick up an envelope containing several hundred dollars in cash at the home of my first client. I was told to open it after I left the house, go to the post office, buy a money order for one hundred dollars, leave the check blank, and mail it to a, address in Oregon. I was to buy a beeper with some of the remaining money and to call her back when I had completed all of this. When I called, she told me she approved of my performance and the fact I did not ask any questions. She told me I was hired.

Who was I to ask questions? I needed some money and a place to live. I was just grateful to have some cash! First I had to digest the reality of the profession. I was going to be a call girl. I was going to go to bed for cold hard cash and I couldn't let my emotions surface. Strangely, after I was hired, I really didn't feel I had any emotions left anyway. It was as if I had just zippered shut that side of me.

One of my first assignments was to visit a local man at his home and give him whatever he asked for. I was amazed that after the transaction was completed, Randy Miller just wanted to talk. He was thrilled I was well traveled and he could communicate with me. We hit it off. "Do you need anything besides money?" he asked.

"Yes," I exclaimed, "I need a room for me and my cat!"

"Consider it done and move in tomorrow," he said immediately.

After tripping over a very large shotgun sticking out from under his bed, I found his ID card one night and discovered his real name was not

Miller and that he was a CIA agent who passed as a travel agent. I never questioned him on the subject. 'When I moved in, he insisted I keep my job; he would do all the cooking for both of us or we would eat out. He didn't want me to cook in his kitchen, and I never could figure that one out. He just seemed happy and content to be in charge of everything. His only request was that I continue to be a charming and willing sex partner and not to interfere with his drinking. He was a serious but highly functioning, responsible alcoholic, who are few and far between.

My last drink of choice before I had quit drinking had been vodka. He kept copious amounts of vodka in the freezer. I believe it was truly a miracle that I didn't want to drink it. He asked me not to bring any drugs into his house or use drugs in his home. We had an understanding and I did not violate it. He wanted me to go about my business and to mind my own business while doing so. I never was a good judge of character, but this man never lied to me that I know of, and he never stiffed me. He asked me to trust him, and I did.

I continued with my job as a call girl. 'Within a couple of weeks, I had put enough money aside to get my own place. I moved out, but because this man and I really liked each other, he often asked me to join him at a bar in the early evening where I would drink non-alcoholic beer. Often I would join him for dinner. I was usually busier in the late hours. It didn't bother him that I was tied to my beeper. He had one as well. I continued to service Randy, but I gave him a discount. He paid me only $100 when the going rate was $200. A client who wanted me for the entire evening paid $400, but the madam always got fifty percent of what I made.

Wally would occasionally come into the bar Randy and I frequented. He was surprised I had moved out of Randy's home, because he knew I had free room and board. I never told Wally anything about this man or what I was doing to make a living. Randy, who as a CIA agent had seen it all, observed that Wally was cheap because he never reciprocated in buying drinks. 'Wally was an odd character; despite his expensive taste in antiques and rare collectibles, he was a crude person who made few friends, Wally did eventually apologize for throwing me out and told me he wasn't surprised I was surviving. Having known me since 1978, he told me he knew I would make it. I kept Wally at a distance since I didn't want anything I did to be any business of his again. He had all of my beautiful bedroom furniture, so he was happy.

Once again I was on my own. I was more content than I had been in a very long time. I accomplished this peace by splitting myself. One part of me handled selling sex for money easily since I was so used to stuffing my emotions. All I had to do was not think about it and go forward. The other part of me, the Roman Catholic side that knew selling sex was an unforgivable sin, was observing my actions, fearful for my soul and my self-esteem. That part of me dreaded the punishment I was sure would come. But I was not punished and life was not as impossible as I thought it would be.

Soon my luck changed drastically. One of my clients names was linked to some underhanded dealings. He asked, as part of his bargaining with the vice squad, if he could turn me in as evidence instead of himself.

On a quiet spring afternoon, two plainclothes policemen came to my door with this client. I could tell by the looks on these men's faces, and from the nervousness of the client, that I had trouble. For several weeks someone had been taking money in advance from the clients, but no call girl had shown up for the clients. The police had caught the driver, who was collecting the money, with a list of names. On this list were the names of the men who had been shortchanged. My client was the only person on that list the police could locate to subpoena. My client claimed his political position would be jeopardized if he were subpoenaed. I didn't know this man's position and I had never asked because I felt it was safer for me nor to know any of the details.

The police asked me for other clients' names. I told them I only, know one name and I was hesitant to give it to them, as this man was my pal. The last thing I wanted was to betray my friend Randy.

"You'd better give it to me, or I will have to handcuff you and take you downtown," one of the officers said.

"Okay, I'll tell you," I said and told them Randy's name. The handcuffs were put away and when the client who had accompanied them was released, he scurried away like a rat.

The officers didn't leave. "How would you like to work undercover for us? We'd really like to reel in your boss. We know she's got several different names and she's a wanted felon." Did I really have a choice? I didn't think so! Would she have me killed if she found out? Probably...

I managed to continue working with both my phone and my beeper bugged. I was under constant surveillance, and it got to the point where I looked for the officers just to chat. I knew I was treading on thin ice and that they could do anything they pleased with me if they turned on me. People had turned on me all of my life, but for a while I just didn't care, I was feeling depressed, alone and friendless. It was a miserable existence and it wasn't getting me anywhere except more deeply entwined with some pretty pathetic people.

Finally I decided to do something more positive, and I entered nursing school to become a certified nursing assistant. I had started as a call girl in January, had gotten caught in March, and registered for nurse's training in April. I felt if I could focus on getting on with my life, even though I was still working as a call girl, then I could become "someone" again. The Oregon woman I worked for was very close to being in the custody of police vice officers, so it was time for a change. It was a blessing that my hours all worked out so well. I could study, work, and attend school on a fulltime basis. I was even able to get enough rest to keep my thinking straight.

Being a call girl was not the difficult job one would imagine. With fewer clients, I was able to focus on my studies and my opportunity for a new life. It's a mystery to me how it all worked out. Every day I prayed that God would forgive me for breaking His laws. I would try to put one foot down and hope my other foot followed. I was not worried about money, as it seemed I always had just enough; however, now I was careful how I spent my money. Some days I would only have two or three dollars, then get a bill in the mail. It was strange, but somehow the bills got paid. If I had some extra money, I knew it would be needed to pay for something important. There never seemed to be any "extra" money ever.

One day the police vice department called and told me that "the madam" was in prison. I had never seen her, so my job was over. They encouraged me to continue working with them on a new drug case, but I could only see my demise if I continued. I expected that I would probably not be so lucky the next time! By now, I had graduated from my nursing course. I had just enough money to get out of Sarasota.

Of course, I could not tell a soul I was going to make my exit. I called the friend in Fort Lauderdale who was the sea captain and asked if he would let me sleep on his sofa until I found a nursing job. He would be in Ft. Lauderdale for a while, and it felt good to have a place to stay with a friend on a temporary basis. I called a moving company and arranged for them to pick up my things in my apartment and put them into storage on the west coast of Florida. The movers came early on a Tuesday morning and I had my phone disconnected that day as well as the TV cable company. It was one plan in my life that didn't backfire. I didn't well a soul and was safe and sound at my friend's apartment in Fort Lauderdale that night. My furniture was safely put away and the chaotic life in Sarasota was over. It was September 1993, the fall of the year I learned how to bend and not break.

17

Faith and Love

All of my hard work and nurse's training paid off when I located a job working for a hospice in Fort Lauderdale from eight in the morning until four in the afternoon. It really suited my nature to work with the dying. I felt it was my calling because I did not find dying to be depressing as some people do. I had had a great deal of experience with death in my family. Dying is as much a part of living as aging. When I was a young girl, a college classmate of my father's told me that one should perfect the art of aging "gracefully." I now believe that one should also die "gracefully." I bought and studied many books on dying, but I did not find it as complicated as so many want to make it. We must die. It is a fact of life.

People don't like to die alone, so I had a job. I was there to make life easier for this final stage of existence on this plane. I felt every Patient who came my way was unique and in my life for some specific reason. Maybe as I get closer to my time to die, I will understand why we have these particular roles to play while we are still alive here on this earth. I am a firm believer in reincarnation, we need to move forward and upward on this plane of living. If we don't try to learn and try to change our wrong ways, then we are coming back here to learn the same lessons we didn't learn the first time around. I was not taught to believe this way by anyone. It is something I firmly believe because it is deeply ingrained, for whatever reason.

It seems to me that the most important lesson to learn here on earth is compassion. There are endless things to be said about the beauty of compassion. Nothing mends a hurt like true compassion. Standing in someone else's moccasins and feeling their feelings is compassion. It takes away the sting in so many situations and mends misunderstandings. I also firmly believe that once we are on the right track with our lives, then death becomes a beautiful experience of our being absorbed by God and the cosmos. We will soar out of our earthly bodies and whirl upward until we are one with God and the heavens.

One day the sea captain, who had loaned me his couch, told me his mother was coming to stay for a month and asked me to "please move on." By this time, I had just enough money saved up to get my furniture out of storage in Sarasota and move it to Fort Lauderdale. I also had the money for a security deposit and for the first and last months rent to put into my own apartment. I mean, I had "exactly" the amount needed—to the penny.

I found a charming one-bedroom apartment that was part of a one-story apartment complex. It had a front yard and a patio in the back with French doors and lots of trees. To me, it seemed like a little house. It was a dream come true! I actually could plant a garden! However, I also knew I could use some help with the rent, as I was just starting my hospice job and my finances were tight. The salary for a nursing assistant was not plentiful.

On the morning I was waiting for the movers to call me, I was still at the sea captains apartment. I looked at the newspaper and saw that he had turned to the "personals." An ad caught my eye. It was simple and undemanding. These ads usually ask for specifics such as a desired height, weight, age and other requirements. But this man was simply looking for a "middle-aged woman." I could deal with that! I copied down the address where I could write to him. When I was finished with my unpacking and settled in my new home later that week, it seemed like the ideal time to contact him. I wrote a brief note stating that I would enjoy meeting him for a cup of coffee. I explained that we would know if we were compatible in fifteen minutes. I had mailed my note and since some time had passed, I had forgotten about it when this "mystery" man called me. He invited me to join him at a restaurant we both knew in Fort Lauderdale. We agreed to meet at the Floridian early Saturday evening, December 11, 1993.

In the meantime, my friends Terry and Merle invited me to the Fort Lauderdale Christmas Pageant at the First Baptist church for that Friday night, December the 10th. Terry and Merle met me in front of the church and gave me a ticket. This enormous church seats 2,450 and is known for their Christmas pageant, which is broadcast on national TV during the Christmas season. The audience seemed excited about the performance but I had no idea what to expect. My seat was located near a cameraman who was very intent on capturing the performance. I was flabbergasted when it started because it felt like being at a Broadway musical. I was surprised when the show started without religious overtones. It was secular, jovial, and festive.

In the second part of the program, after Jesus was born, I was mesmerized by what happened next. To the music of "Silent Night," the actors playing shepherds and peasants, each bearing a candle, slowly and quietly walked one by one from the back of the church down the church aisles toward the stage and the manger. The actors walked right by me, enhancing my feelings of awe. I saw a sandaled foot step near me, and when I looked up, for a second I thought I saw Jesus. At that very minute, I understood what it took for me to be a Christian. I was to walk in those sandals and to try to act like Jesus! The impact was so strong that the rest of the performance paled in comparison to the effect that moment had on me. From that moment on I wanted to be a Christian in every way and I knew it would be a long hard road. I wondered how I was going to cope with trying to live up to what I believe was expected of me.

The next morning I was elated from feeling true Christmas spirit. Michael, the gentleman I was scheduled to meet that afternoon, called to confirm our date. I could tell that my Christmas spirit was contagious as I related the previous evenings performance to him. His tone became more excited and he became uplifted.

At five-thirty I entered the Floridian and spotted an eager, redheaded man with a bushy red beard and a pipe, just as Michael had described himself He was sitting at a table in the center of the restaurant and stood up as he watched me. "Hi, I'm Joni," I said as I walked up to him.

"Hi, I'm Mike," he said with a Missouri twang as he smiled broadly at me. I immediately felt drawn to him by his firm handshake and his bright blue eyes that fixed on me.

"Hello, Michael," I replied. I had right away decided that his name was too wonderful to be abbreviated. I took in and approved of the classic style of the Navy blue blazer he was wearing. He looked me over and I could see he was impressed with my cream-colored jacket and my long, colorful tropical print skirt.

My instincts told me Michael was my next "mission." At that time in my life, I felt that all the men I was meeting had some deep-seated pain that needed to be healed with love and nurturing. I'm sure some of those feelings were left over from my days as a flight attendant or nurse, always trying to help and please others. I was "Miss People Pleaser". Something also told me our relationship was going to be a difficult, rewarding, yet lasting experience. The very nature of my thoughts surprised me, as I hadn't focused on anything but survival in a very long while.

When I was seated, the waiter asked me what I would like to drink. I hadn't had a drink in four years and told him I would like a non-alcoholic beer.

"Why did you order a non-alcoholic beer?" Michael asked me.

"I'm an alcoholic," I answered.

"What a coincidence! I am too," Michael said with a smile. "We're both alcoholics in recovery. Bravo for us!" This coincidence amazes us to this day.

"What do you do for a living?" I asked him.

"I've just returned from two years of cruising in the Caribbean and I loved every minute of it. My father, brothers and I owned a boatyard in Lighthouse Point, Florida, for twenty years," Michael explained. "I branched out on my own and became a marine surveyor. Every day people would tell me about their cruising adventures, and I started to dream about doing that myself. I wanted to do some serious cruising aboard my own boat, and my dream came true.""

"I've done some cruising too, but I'm grateful to have cruising out of my system," I told him. I *thought* I understood him to say he was glad he also had cruising out of his system. "I lost everything due to my quest for the perfect sunset during my sailing venture," I admitted.

Had I suspected he wasn't actually finished with the cruising life and boating, I would have finished my drink, wished him well, thanked him for the beer and conversation, and left in a hurry to return home. It was through this basic misunderstanding that our relationship began. Instantly we had both lowered our guards and were open to each other. He asked me to join him for supper that night, and we went to a Chinese restaurant on Las Olas Boulevard. During our meal, we chattered like two monkeys in a banana tree! Since that time, I have realized that a man may think he's finished with the sea, but the sea is finished with the man only when the sea decides-nor the man! We humans are powerless when it comes to the sea and her mystery.

Michael won my heart when he bought me a cappuccino and we strolled along the boulevard looking in the shop windows. "Tell me more about yourself " Michael asked as we walked along.

"I've had an adventurous life. My parents lived in Europe when I was a child and I loved getting to know the different cultures, especially Spain. But we also lived in France and Germany. I'd like to go back to Europe and see it all again. And not only Europe. I've always wanted to see Greece, and I think it would be terrific to work on a kibbutz in Israel."

"How lucky you were to do so much traveling," Michael enthused. "I've never been to Europe, but I d love to go. Maybe we could go together."

We are both adventurous individuals and were thrilled to find each other. He saw me home and then returned the next morning for Sunday services at the Baptist church where I had recently seen the Christmas pageant. After Michael left me that afternoon, I knew we had something very special and that we were in each other's lives for a specific purpose. I was pretty surprised that my Higher Power had pulled me through so much chaos and now presented me with a nice and gentle recovering alcoholic.

Christmas was just around the corner. I was still working for the hospice and was sure I was in the right profession. I was working in the home of an elderly woman dying of congestive heart failure. She was very sweet but demanded her privacy. She had a little crystal bell beside her bed that she would ring when she needed me.

On Friday I had my first "real" date with Michael. When he asked what I wanted to do, I told him all I wanted was to take a long walk and eat a frozen yogurt. I didn't want a heavy meal and the walk would give me the opportunity to find out more about him.

Michael and I discovered we had more in common—he had also been married several times, but he was the father to two grown sons he had helped raise. He was quite the sailor; he had owned more than thirty boats and had spent most of his summers cruising the Bahamas. Before the evening ended, he wanted me to see his boat, where he was currently living.

Before we went onboard, I practically froze to the dock because his boat was a thirty-seven-footer as mine had been. When he showed me around, however, I thought his boat's interior layout wasn't as comfortable as mine had been. Although I could sense we would make good sailing partners, I was torn. Part of me wanted to escape and cruise to the South Pacific, but the other part remembered how awful it was trying to sail my own boat. So many things had gone wrong for me. I was really exhausted from living a gypsy lifestyle; I wanted to finally put down some roots.

I'll never forget that Friday because it was also the day I found out my HIV test results were negative, and I was so relieved. I had had visions of contracting AIDS through my call girl days in Sarasota. That chapter was finally over—the worst year of my life was done and finished. I felt I could breathe more deeply and see more clearly. Life was suddenly very different and positive for me. I had hope!

Michael and I were both ready to establish a relationship and we saw each other almost daily. Because we were so compatible, our relationship developed quickly into a routine, almost like we were already married. Since we saw each other all the time, he offered to help me financially and gave me money to buy groceries and help with the rent. To me he was everything I needed and wanted in a relationship, the answer to my prayers.

Even though I realized I could move aboard his boat and my dream to see the South Pacific would become a reality I dragged my feet. I kept remembering my problems when I had taken off for the Bahamas and the Caribbean ten years before. But here I was, once again living in Fort Lauderdale. I figured that after all the places I had been and all that I had done, God had put me in Fort Lauderdale for a purpose. I believed God's plans were for me to stay right where I was; I was afraid to jump into anything too rash again. By spring of 1994 Michael had committed to me, had sold his boat and moved in with me. I think one of his incentives was my enthusiasm to travel and see the world.

It was a difficult time for me deciding how best to worship the Higher Power in my life. Both Michael and I needed to be spiritually fed. Although I enjoyed the Baptist church and had even brought Michael to the Lutheran church, he didn't feel comfortable in either place. One Sunday Michael's brother invited us to attend Calvary Chapel, a non-denominational church. We chose to attend for the time being because we found that the minister was terrific and inspiring.

During church service one Sunday, Michael went forward to ask God to forgive him of his sins and to turn his life over to Jesus. When someone goes forward in a church setting in a moment of passion, it seems so easy to change one's ways immediately. However, to change is progressive. It is like picking up a white chip at an AA meeting and saying, "I will surrender my way of living and start a new way of life." Change has to happen one day at a time- sometimes, one hour at a time, or even minute by minute. It is a slow process and there is a program to follow. In Christianity the Program is to follow Jesus' example and the Bible's teachings. Michael seemed ready at this moment in 7994 to begin his new way of life. He is still a committed Christian. I am impressed how focused he is on the Bible. He reads it daily and is a member of a men's Bible study group in his quest to understand how and where he fits into the Christian scheme of things.

Faith is a process. I continue my process to understand my own picture of faith and began my own serious search for spirituality. What I was practicing might have been confusing to some since I was attending different churches, but it was my own way of serving my unique needs. I attended Mass every weekday morning during the Lenten season since I needed to touch base with my Roman Catholic roots. I once again began to feel comfortable at Mass. I understand about Jesus when I receive communion because during Mass the sacrifice of Christ's death on the cross is underlined. His death for me was so that I might know everlasting life after my earthly death on this plane. This belief is the bottom line of my faith.

One day I decided to go to confession at the Roman Catholic Church. I had not been since the '70s. I had not gone near a Catholic priest because I felt intense anger at Brent's 1979 annulment of our marriage in the Roman Catholic Church. I needed to get right with God and tell everything to the priest, from my being a mistress to being a call girl. I had years and years of a lifestyle lacking in morals bottled up inside me. Alcoholics

Anonymous encourages us to admit our shortcomings to another human being as part of the recovery process. I had the Ten Commandments and the Seven Deadly Sins to deal with, and I had violated them ALL-Pride, Anger, Greed, Sloth, Gluttony, Lust and Envy. I just let the priest have it all, and he helped me to let go and turn it all over to my Higher Power.

After my confession, the priest said I was forgiven and told me not to repeat those sins again. I went from the confessional into the church to pray. I thought I heard the words, "Be still and know that I am God." Why would I hear that? I'd never heard those words before. 'Where did those words come from and what could they mean? I knew in my heart it was God who asked me to "be still." I interpreted that to mean I needed to wait for an outcome, so I waited.

Michael presented me with an emerald and diamond ring not long afterward. He told me he was committed to the relationship and wanted to marry me, so on June 11th, we announced our engagement. We had met on December 11th, so this was exactly six months since the day we had met. We called Michaels parents and told them the news. We decided to make eleven a special number for us, so we planned our wedding for September 11th, 1994.

On October 11, we left for our honeymoon in Spain and Greece. We arrived in Madrid early on the morning of the 12th. We were flying standby and were unable to continue on to Athens because all the flights were fully booked due to a Spanish holiday. We found a hotel in downtown Madrid, and we got mugged when we went out for a walk later that night! Five gypsies took Michaels wrist pouch containing our travelers checks and his passport. One of them cut Michaels arm in his haste to cut off the pouch's strap. During the attack I curled up into a ball and hung onto my purse. I didn't think about what they could do to me but I screamed and screamed. I just knew I could not give up my purse because it contained my medicine. Being a manic- depressive, I would have had to return to my doctor in Fort Lauderdale for medicine, which would mean forsaking our honeymoon. The very core of my being would not give up! I was rolled around, kicked and tugged at, but I managed to hold onto my purse until the police came.

The police did nothing except ask us if we could identify our attackers, which was impossible because of the crowds. Due to the holiday, the streets were full of celebrators. I don't recall seeing the robbers' faces, but since Michael had been held at knifepoint, he had looked into their eyes. Later, he told me the man who had cut his arm had the eyes and expression of the devil. These men were gypsies and that is all we knew. We just wanted to get out of Spain at this point! The next morning we were faced with recovering our passports and traveler's checks. We met another couple at the American Embassy, who had been mugged as well. We ended up joining them for lunch and later for dinner that night and were finally able to enjoy Madrid. The following morning we decided to pay full fare to get to Barcelona, the only way we could get out of Madrid.

In Barcelona we once again took a chance with flying stand-by on Iberia Airlines to Athens. Much to our surprise, we got a fight in Barcelona and were greatly relieved, as it was a non-stop fight. We arrived in Athens early in the evening. We had no idea where to begin looking for accommodations, but our taxi driver suggested a hotel. Curiosity got the best of us, so we consented, and it turned out to be the perfect hotel for us! The room we got was small, but it had a balcony and a bathroom and it was clean. For about a week we stayed at this hotel; during the day we walked all around the charming Place neighborhood and took day and nighttime tours of Athens and the surrounding countryside. To complete our trip, we took a cruise through the Greek Islands. It was a splendid, magical honeymoon made more special by our fondness for Greek people, Greek music and Greek food. Since Michael is fascinated with archaeology, some locations, like the island of Patmos where Saint John wrote the Book of Revelation, were a real treat for him.

One morning during the island cruise we woke up very early and found the dining room empty. Michael went to the lovely breakfast buffet and had his usual cereal and milk as a starter. I sipped my coffee and enjoyed waking up slowly. By nine we were STILL the only ones in the dining room. By ten, still alone, we felt like we were in the "Twilight Zone."

"Why are we the only ones here?" we asked the steward. When he gave us a strange look we asked again.

"Last night," he finally told us in excellent English, "there was an awful storm, one of the worst I have experienced myself. All the passengers were awake and seasick all night long. Because they were afraid and angry, they were threatening all the crew. Of course now they are all in their cabins recovering."

We both laughed. No wonder we had slept so well-it was the rough weather. The sea tossing the ship about was a familiar and soothing sensation for us. We are both sailors to the core!

18

A Major Setback

In spite of my two years of marriage to Michael and the stability it offered me, I was slowly beginning to feel devastating emotional pain. For the first time in my life, I was trying to bond with my husband and with my friends, but I was having great difficulty developing closeness to anyone. For years I had anaesthetized myself with alcohol and when I awoke in sobriety, I discovered all my faults, all the things missing in my life, like close emotional bonds with other people, including my current husband. I had never been able to develop close bonds since my breakup with Brent, my first husband. My efforts to get close to people did not feel comfortable for me; the feelings scared me. I did not know how to trust or bond and began having anxiety attacks more and more often. I felt hollow and lost and didn't know what to do about it.

I had been seeing a woman therapist since I had moved back to Fort Lauderdale in 1993. My sessions were part of my recovery process and a follow up for my manic depressive disorder. I needed to talk out my emotional mood swings with her, and had to keep remembering that alcoholism is an emotional disorder. With manic-depression, it is helpful for me to talk to a mental health professional regularly, because often it is difficult for me to recognize an oncoming manic episode. It is helpful to hear myself talk out loud when I am approaching one of these episodes. During a "high" episode manic-depressives begin to think irrationally and often become delusional. And when the depressions become overwhelming g and paralyzing, it's good to have someone there for support. All of this goes hand in hand with knowing how much and when to take the necessary medications for this disease.

My therapist, who I'd been seeing for quite a while, was a licensed social worker. One day, out of the blue, she suggested I try sipping two glasses of wine a day in an effort to cope with things. At first it sounded like I was hearing things! My rational self-wanted to deny that this woman was malicious. How could someone so aware of my struggle for sobriety suggest such a thing? But the seed had been planted and there is nothing more alluring to an alcoholic than permission to take a drink!

I overlooked the warnings AA had given me. Friends in the AA program suggested I avoid hanging around alcoholics who were actively drinking. I had three friends who had each been in the AA program for eight years. They were all now out of the program and were drinking alcohol. I didn't want to admit I was making a big mistake by remaining on close terms with these women. I saw them as being nonchalant about their drinking behavior, and I was determined to be as successful as they were at drinking. What I did not see was their inner emotional pain and the fact that drinking was not solving their problems. They never told me their problems, as if they didn't have any. I didn't see how their lives were slowly becoming unmanageable because I had never seen them drunk or out of control. I later discovered how wrong I was. Looking back, I now realize the relationship I had with my God, as I knew Him, was slipping away, and I was slowly losing my faith.

I had conveniently forgotten that alcohol had taken me into poverty and poor judgment with my life in general. I had forgotten I could not drink successfully. I had forgotten I had lost EVERYTHING, including my pride, dignity and spirituality. With my pancreatitis, I had also almost lost my life.

One day I was with one of these drinking friends getting ready to go to the beach. We were stocking our cooler with wine and champagne, and I decided to fix a drink for the road. I quickly put together a "short" Bloody Mary. Down deep I knew I needed to avoid that first drink. It had been my drink of choice before I entered the treatment center and the world of AA. I didn't think about whether or not I could handle it; it was as if I had totally shut out my logical thinking! When we were in the car and on our way to the beach, I took a sip. That very first drink made me almost scream, "This is the answer to the puzzle!" It was all I could do to contain myself. "Reality' hit me square between the eyes. I realized that all of this time it was the hard liquor I had been craving because of the numbness that accompanied it. It's strong and it's quick.

During the whole time we were at the beach, my mind was consumed with the thought that I had tasted my true addiction. It hit me that I had been playing mind games with myself I had been sober for seven years, and yet there was still something irresistible about drinking vodka. When I drink it, I literally escape into that numb dimension. I'm not sure if this is what happens with other alcoholics, but it certainly happens for me. It alters my state of awareness and changes my state of mind. Alcohol is a mind-altering substance.

After that trip to the beach I decided not to drink vodka again, but I did continue to sneak wine. I avoided speaking to any of the people I knew in AA. I was withdrawing from humanity and returning to my old habit of isolating. During this time, I was house-sitting daily at a home on the water in Fort Lauderdale. The owners lived in Arizona. The refrigerator was well stocked with the finest of- all the vodkas. There was even a pepper-flavored vodka. Every day when I checked on the house, I looked to see if the pepper-flavored vodka w:rs there. It was safe and sound in the fridge. Each day I made the conscious decision to have wine instead of vodka. The wine did take the edge off my emotional discomfort.

The vodka was another story, offering me freedom from life and my painful existence. Yes, it would be suicide. Vodka was like a gun or a knife because it represented death to me. I thought it would save me from myself' However, I just didn't have the strength for a slow death anymore, as I did when I was dying of pancreatitis in 1988. I wanted another dimension I could escape to; I didn't want to be alive. Somewhere in the recesses of my mind, I knew that life didn't have to feel this awful, but I didn't know what to do about it.

Volumes of literature have been devoted to understanding the nature of the alcoholic. I am an alcoholic, and I know that I drink because I have fear. While I am drinking, I know no fear. I had held a job that dealt with people and their fear of flying, crashing, and dying. But I had never clarified or identified the sources of my many fears. I had never permitted myself to investigate that area of my mind while working as a flight attendant. Drinking alcohol for the alcoholic is both a mental and a physical obsession. We keep on swallowing and consuming the alcohol in order to deal with our fear and emotional pain. There is a continuous craving that accompanies that first drink. I drink alcohol to get away from reality I go to another plane of existence in order to COPE with whatever pain I can't deal with at the time. This pain can be people whom I cannot tolerate, an overwhelming job, or a difficult situation. All of the things that cause us to retreat into the bottle are driven by fear, shame, hurt or disappointments. I realize that I need to know I am an acceptable person. This longing for acceptance is felt by most alcoholics.

When I was drunk, I didn't care about the fears or emotional pain. I had to learn that drinking made anything I did or the way I felt much wor. se. I needed the Alcoholic Anonymous program to show me how to accept myself as I am in a sober state. Alcoholism is an emotional disease and is a VERY insidious disorder. The only answer for me is complete abstinence fr.om alcohol. Taking up hungover and shaky after having "blackouts" at social gatherings is unacceptable behavior. I had wrecked cars and relationships throughout the years, and this behavior caused me much shame when I was sober. Worst of all, while I drank I had no relationship with myself or with my true spirit.

There is a point in time in the state of recovery that makes us feel as though we are on a "pink cloud." This pink cloud experience is a good calm feeling that happens when the urge to drink leaves us. Everything seems to work like clockwork. I hadn't experienced this pink cloud in so long I couldn't remember what the people in AA were talking about. I had forgotten what it was like to be content with myself and at peace with the world, and what it was like to accept what I couldn't change in life-the very gift of acceptance. For me, my life was still like a clawing in my soul that made me want to be drunk and oblivious to everything.

Before this bout of drinking I had had seven years and two months of sobriety. The reality of trying to bond with another person in a genuine and sober way had become a tremendously overwhelming threat to me.

Not having developed a relationship with myself I was extremely fearful of intimacy. In November of 1995 I picked up a drink to deliver me from this painful reality. I withdrew from Michael and left him alone with the mental anguish of trying to connect with me. I didn't drink in the open; I was sneaking off and drinking alone and even Michael didn't know what was wrong with me. 'When I returned to the AA meetings, the only people who were able to accept me were the ones who had had the same experience of a relapse. It was then I realized I needed to try not to drink. I had to try not to drink just for the day. I could NOT look into the future at the fact that I could NEVER drink again. This was just too difficult and arduous to accomplish, so I continued to drink secretly over the next four months. Alcohol had beaten me again.

19

The Miraculous Healing Power of Hope and Faith

I somehow knew that in order to cope with my fears I had to build an inner strength and honesty deeper than I had ever known. Somewhere, way down deep inside my heart and spirit, I realized I had hope that things would and could be better. I started to pray. I was grateful I still had some of my faith; I held onto it so tightly I thought I might crack in two. I prayed that God, in His infinite wisdom, would help me see the complete picture of my life. Life really is a jigsaw puzzle, and at that moment all I had was "one" piece of the puzzle—I had hope. Thinking about it more and more, I realized I had always been hopeful, maybe just a small glimmer, but I had held it once in my grip. I had seen a small light at the end of the tunnel in 1967 when I met Brent at Harvard, and he taught me how to believe in myself. Now it was 1997, and I had almost forgotten how Brent taught me to believe I could have anything I wanted. My biggest problem has always been believing in myself identifying my goals and pursuing them.

I remembered being at Mass with my father in St. Patriclis Cathedral in New York City on Easter Sunday in 1976. We had just buried my mother. We were kneeling in our pew when I noticed the entire cathedral was decorated with yellow forsythias. The sight was so lovely it almost took my breath away. My father told me that forsythia is the first flower of spring. He also said, "This is the flower of hope because spring and the rest of the flowers are coming soon."

It was the memory of that beautiful moment of hope that finally gave me the courage to call my AA sponsor after four months of drinking. That courage seemed to come from an energy I like to think of as my Higher Power. When my sponsor heard my voice, she said, "something is wrong and I want to know what it is NOW!"

"I'm sorry to say I've been drinking," I said softly.

She was silent for a moment and then said, "You need to pick up a white chip and start all over, right NOW!" She had me meet her immediately at one of the AA clubhouses and we attended a meeting together. There comes a moment of reality in everyone's life that is of particular importance. At that meeting I realized I had the chance of taking charge of my life again, but it was now or absolutely never. My sponsor looked me in the eye with such intensity it made me shudder. She had the eyes of a marksman. Her look told me she had one bullet left, and she would not miss her target.

This was my *last* chance. For the first time in thirty years, I felt I could identify my goal. It was to go forward, NOT backward, ever again. That day was March 11, 1997. I picked up what I hope will be my last white chip. Of course, the AA policy is not to think of sobriety as final, but to take it **one** day at a time. That is all, **one** day and that is it. It is human nature to complicate this advice and to go against it, but the Bible does say to ask only for "Our Daily Bread."

Starting over was difficult, but in the long run, so good for me. It was humbling to return to AA, which meant admitting I was making another attempt at sobriety and the necessity of surrendering. However, this time I was much more centered because I had a loving husband-possessive, but loving. I also had a sense of security and a tad more self-confidence. I had isolated myself from others in the past and denied all my inner feelings and emotions, but now I realized isolation leads to loneliness and loneliness for me can lead to depression, or even worse.

I had to work on my faith. My belief system had functioned like a network of sorts. First I had been a Roman Catholic, then a Lutheran. I got baptized by submersion in the Baptist Church and finally returned to the Catholic Church again-all in an effort to strengthen my faith. I joined a women's nondenominational course called Bible Study Fellowship to gain more knowledge of God's Word. Studying the Bible gave me quite a bit of insight into how Jesus Christ could fit into my life if I was going to call myself a Christian. This nine-month Bible course took a great deal of determination and included many hours of extensive and tedious homework.

Two thousand years ago Jesus came into this world and tried to teach us how to love one another. Many people, and even some Christian churches, want to complicate His simple teachings about how we need to love and forgive one another and need to develop true compassion for others. At the end of the course I was able to determine that faith is a gift. It is a gift I readily accept. Alcoholics who are actively drinking block the ability to receive this gift. I believe God is very selective as to who receives this gift of faith. If He has offered us this gift over and over again, and we deny it continuously, then it is no wonder our hearts are hardened and we find ourselves unable to believe! Faith is a continuous process of realizing how we fit into the picture *with God daily*. For me, this faith was another miracle along with my sobriety.

The classes were helpful, but finally I had to shed all of my book knowledge and go with my gut feelings and experiences. I had to go back in time. I remembered what my father had taught me when I was a little girl. One night when I was quite young, he tried to explain God to me. During an electrical storm when I was extremely frightened and crying because of the lightning and thunder, he told me the universe is made up of positive and negative forces and that the result is electricity and energy, thus Life. My father held me on his lap and hugged me; he pointed to the storm and said that it was God's essence. At that time, I thought God must be angry if He had to make such a noisy and bright display of His feelings. God frightened me as a child and I felt uncomfortable about Him. I thought He must be awfully big, quite terrible, and very angry. During my Catholic school years, I was taught I would have to pay BIG TIME if I sinned. Back then, I could never visualize God as a loving and compassionate Father. I needed to realize that Jesus is the essence of compassion. God is an extremely patient, forgiving and merciful Father. He is very aware of our struggles as we search to find Him. He is there and waiting.

Now, years later, I see how my husband keeps his faith very simple by believing that the whole spiritual situation is a "personal" relationship between God and himself. I decided to find my own personal relationship with God. I had to start somewhere, and I chose the beach, which is where I feel, hear, and see the power of the Divine Oneness.

My faith began as a child through knowing that God is the source of all energy. At the beach I could actually see this in the ocean and in the rhythm of the waves. I could feel His energy in the wind. When I look up at the sky, I am mesmerized by the clouds changing their forms as if they are living and breathing. I am amazed at the strength of the moon that causes the tides to rise and fall. God is truly the essence of harmony, balance and order in the universe. There, at the beach, I am in constant awe of the continuous performance taking place around me. I watch the birds. They trust and therefore are taken care of. When we humans enter the picture, it is obvious our selfishness, egos and free will get us into trouble. Sometimes our choices disrupt the natural order in life.

In the wonder of God's ways, I found myself in a yoga class. I was taking yoga to overcome tension in my back and neck. One day, Mark, the instructor, told me to buy *The Quest* by Paramahansa Yogananda and to open the book at random now and then. He told me I would receive the information and guidance I needed from the book when I was feeling troubled or confused. Being me, I couldn't do that. I had to read the book from cover to cover and study it for one year! I thought it was bizarre that I had had the opportunity to read Paramahansa's material in 1981 when I attended an ashram in Calabasas, California. Life would have been so different for me if I had read it then and followed Yoganandas teachings instead of turning to alcohol and a wayward lifestyle. Yogananda devoted his life to God. His books guide people into spiritually, and away from the turmoil of a materialistic existence.

During and after reading The Qwest, I spent months living a very simple life. I made a sincere effort to live within our financial means. I was frugal with Michael's income, my small pension, and my social security disability income. I considered it a bonus when I could get away from the frantic world of the city and go to the beach. I was always prepared for my "beach time," just in case I had ten minutes or more to spare. My beach chair, umbrella and towel were always at the ready. Sometimes in my haste, I wasn't careful where I placed my chair and shoes, and a wave would try to abscond with them! All I wanted to do was understand how I fit into the master plan of God's infinite universe. For me, this is the ultimate mystery of life.

One day while I was on the beach I heard the words, "You need to move out of the way if you want Me to reside in your heart." It was then I realized my faith was stronger than ever and that my pride and ego were in the way. That night I had a dream of being in a fish market. I heard, "I will not be bargained with!" The words were so loud they woke me up.

I bought a book on Mother Teresa's teachings. When I opened it, the first thing I read was, "Seeking the face of God in everything, every one, everywhere, all the time and seeing His hand in every happening-that is contemplation in the heart of the world." That statement made sense to me, and I no longer felt alone. I thought about this very simple woman whose life was uncomplicated. I wanted an uncomplicated life filled with serenity.

The world and all its trickery is always there to tempt me into confusion and self-indulgence. By studying the Bible, I had been put on alert of the powers of the Devil, or Satan. The Evil One is cunning, baffling and powerful, just like alcohol itself. He is always lurking and waiting for us to give him the chance to take control of us. He has nothing better to do than to wait for this opportunity. Because of this fact, I continue to build up my health, to live as simply as possible, to deepen my relationship with Michael, and to be careful to attend to my spiritual life and needs. I have become stronger as a result of continuous perseverance and daily prayer.

I wanted to further develop my feminine side, so I enrolled in a course called "Fascinating Womanhood." This course taught me to lean on Michael and let him take the lead. Up until then, the closest I had ever come to letting any man actually take the lead was on the dance floor. I'm a terrible dancer, so even that was a challenge! I've found the more I let Michael lead, the more I find him consulting me. This is how we began to make decisions together and to learn how to empower each other.

I realized that I had a lot to learn about how to be a wife. I had to learn how to *believe* in Michael and his capabilities as a man. I busied myself trying to make our home warm and loving for both of us. Now I make a point to discuss anything that involves the two of us. 'We share financial difficulties, personal problems, and social questions. I put down my guard and openly tell him my fears and joys. This sharing has been an important lesson for me because I was accustomed to keeping things to myself and being independent. I was often fearful of rejection or of being let down. I feel there are many people in our independent society who act like I did. They don't how or when to rely on another person for what that person is capable of doing. They don't know what the other person's limits are. Openness, honesty and courtesy don't come automatically to everyone. It takes time to learn how to nurture and cultivate a relationship. It can cause extreme discomfort and embarrassment when we try to relay our pain to an unfeeling partner.

Since Michael was my fourth husband, you might think I should have known how to go about married life—*not so!!!* am also Michaels fourth wife, and he wasn't any more prepared to live a successful marriage than I was. Sometimes I feel it would help us if we both had a Ph.D. in business, home economics and definitely psychology. Our life together might be easier and less complicated! Marital success does not evolve without work and sacrifice on each spouse's part. Both Michael and I can attest to that. Sometimes it is the hardest work we ever do because it comes from inside—from our souls and our hearts. The most important things for us to have in our relationship are complete honesty respect and trust. Honesty, respect and trust all go hand in hand.

I'm finding out that marriage is like a delicate, fragile young plant needing constant nurturing, patience and tender loving care. I feel that Michael has been placed in my life for me to learn how to develop a strong relationship and how to be a good companion. He is experiencing the same with me. Michael has always been satisfied with me except when I withdrew into myself and found it too difficult to communicate. He was shattered when I drank during the winter of 1997.It devastated him because he loved me just the way I was before I drank. Michael was willing to accept me sober, but not as an unhappy drunk.

Now understand when I took that first drink again, my self-esteem was very low. I felt I needed to act out that low opinion as if I were destined to be a drunk. It was all I knew how to do. I was disillusioned with being a retired flight attendant with no developed skills or qualifications other than how to evacuate airplanes and give emergency medical treatment and how to quickly serve trays and drinks to masses of people. As a certified nursing assistant, I wasn't able to hold a serious, medically-oriented job because the more highly trained professionals were sought after.

The more I learn about marriage, the more I realize it is not for everyone. Some people just *cannot* live with another person, which is not a bad thing. It is a very giving experience to live side by side with someone. A great deal of tolerance and patience is needed because there is always one's mate to consider. Marriage is an intimate partnership between two people.

I also realize that children are not for everyone either. It can be sheer agony for someone who doesn't have the patience for children. To rear a child is a career in itself, I think that by nature people are selfish, and raising a child is primarily a selfless experience, or should be one. I'm so grateful I realized I wasn't cut out for the role of parenting while I was young, before I made the mistake of thinking I could attempt such an awesome responsibility. I have trouble controlling myself so there would have been mayhem if I had had a child or two. So many of my friends have told me how happy their lives are because of their children. These friends have strong, healthy, adoring children and plenty of time to give to their offspring. I was just too afraid that if I had had children, they would not have had a strong start because "I" was so mixed up from the beginning.

Life, I know is a series of continuous lessons. For me the greatest lesson has been to learn how to accept myself and eventually love myself, Life continues, and so do the lessons, just as the sun rises and then sets. These lessons are as perennial as the years going by. However, for an alcoholic, it must NOT stop there. I am "daily" trying to work the program of Alcoholics Anonymous. I need to call my sponsor daily. I continue to attend the meetings offered by AA. And it *still* doesn't end here. I had to spend a year on the twelve steps with my sponsor. Fortunately, she had the time to invest in me as I struggled. I have the Bible of AA the *Big Book* to guide me. I need to know what it says. The meetings and the literature need attention. These things are habits for *self-preservation*. The *Big Book* explains the alcoholic, alcoholism and addiction like no other book in this world. It is my lifesaver. It is even helpful for those outsiders who are curious about the disease or have someone they love involved with an addiction.

I realize my life has been a miracle. The Alcoholics Anonymous slogan, "Don't give up before the miracle," has a deep sense of meaning for me. I have come a long, long way from being a stranded, lonely, dying drunk onboard my leaky old boat. Those days of drunkenness and misery seem a very long way away at this time in my life.

I know I am very blessed now, as Michael is a devoted husband, a good provider, and my best friend. He has seen me through my challenges and has loved me just as I am. He has gone through hell trying to understand and cope with the insanity involved with my disease of manic-depression. It is because of Michael's unfailing and unconditional love that I have been able to lead a somewhat normal life. In essence I've never totally lost my faith, despite the serious ups and downs I have experienced due to my bipolar disorder. There have been very trying times when I have needed to seek out my psychiatrist as often as once or twice a week while whirling through a full-blown manic. Those manics are just about impossible to describe. I am very grateful that my psychiatrist hasn't seen the need to hospitalize me in the past few years. There is such an intense energy level that seems almost inhuman, which accompanies the "highs" of this disorder. There is such agony for me to not be able to sleep for days at a time, even with my medication tripled. I thank God for both my psychiatrist, Dr. de Elejalde and my present therapist, Dr. O'Connor. They have worked so hard with me trying to understand what sometimes translates as gibberish when I try to express myself when I'm too high or too low.

I believe my attempt at spirituality is what has kept me glued together all these years since my first attempt to pray as a sober person. It is so common for the manic-depressive to turn to pot or alcohol, hoping to find some kind of peace. I've suffered from this disorder for almost thirty years and today the medications are so much more effective. Of course, the trick with this disease is *staying* on the drug prescribed by the doctor, as so many patients with this disorder think the worst is over when they level out and start to feel balanced. It is so easy to slowly begin to feel the sense of ecstasy and to eventually become totally delusional and grandiose. The manic state often creeps into our beings so gradually that it is too difficult and often too late to realize what is happening. It is a sneaky, disease.

Recently, I read Dr. Kay Redfield Jamison's book, *An Unquiet Mind.* She said someone described the disease as "rotten luck." She suffers from manic- depression and is one of the lucky ones who didn't have to lose everything.

The moccasins (or deck shoes) I wear have been very high maintenance. I've had to learn how to balance in them and I've come a long way. Some parts of my life have been a terrible struggle, but because of these difficulties, I can better understand the resiliency of the human spirit.

20

Onward and Upwards

Michael and I have always been curious about seeing the worlds different cultures, its famous landmarks and interesting places. We have been blessed by having so many of our dreams come true. We both dreamed of seeing Machu Picchu, the abandoned "Lost City of the Incas" at the top of the Andes mountains in the jungles of Peru. That dream became a reality and it was one of the most marvelous adventures we've ever had! When we arrived in Lim, Peru, it was very hot, like Miami. After exploring Lima, we flew to Cuzco, a heavily populated city in the Andes. In Cuzco we caught the red and yellow train for Machu Picchu and rode the switchbacks to Agua Caliente, the tiny jungle village at the base of the mountains. From there, only one bus at a time can drive the steep and narrow winding road up the mountain to Machu Picchu. The view was unforgettably breathtaking all the way up to the ruins and from the ruins themselves, our trip could only be termed an awesome experience and I almost had to pinch myself to believe that any place could be so beautiful.

Our good fortune has never stopped. We have a dear friend who lives on his canal barge in France. For three summers in a row, he invited us to join him in exploring the canals and rivers of France. His barge was over fifty feet long and he couldn't operate it alone. Michael assisted him as his deckhand as we went through the endless locks along the canals. I did the cooking. It was a delightful challe.ge trying to shop and provision the barge with Food since I have a somewhat limited knowledge of the French language.

We absolutely love the French countryside. The people of rural France lead such a tranquil existence. Even in the most remote village we found at least one or two outdoor cafes. There we sat with the locals and enjoyed a cup of coffee or a cool glass of water. It was the perfect opportunity to relax, watch people, think things over or just enjoy a daydream.

One of the things we love about rural France is that when lunchtime comes, everything closes and *everyone* takes the time for a long, leisurely lunch, a chat and maybe a nap. The French know how to take care of themselves and their loved ones. ti7hen we returned to our home base in South Florida after our vacation in France, we always had a bit of culture shock. Rural France is so much like life in the United States fifty years ago. People in todays cities are usually in a frantic hurry with their self-imposed deadlines and the deadlines of their jobs. In a fast-paced life, there's less time for meditation, reflection and prayer. Michael and I are looking for serenity away from the turmoil found in cities. We find that we go out of our way to avoid people caught up in a chaotic existence.

Michael and I experienced the wonder of love in the summer of 1998 on a tiny island in the Abaco Islands of the Bahamas. We rented a house in the village of Hope Town. It was so magical that we returned to the same island the following year and rented a spacious and comfortable beach house on a ridge overlooking the Atlantic Ocean. It was a special vacation in the lazy, languid style of the Bahamas, surrounded by the breathtaking beauty of the azure sea. The house faced east, so we saw some spectacular sunrises from the porch during the two weeks we were there. 'We were about a mile from the tiny village and Michael walked to town daily for our provisions. The town even had a weekly AA meeting, which we attended. At this meeting we met several delightful people from as far away as Hawaii. 'We played in the sea like children and learned how to keep life simple and how to communicate with each other. The soft sea breeze whispered to us, and we listened to the churning and lapping of the sea as it kissed the shore. I was so still that my self-winding watch stopped working, but it was a beautiful experience not to care what time it was!

As we look to our future, there is much more Michael and I want to do with our lives! The sea and her mystery call to us. Michael missed the sea so much that he hunted for years to find the ideal boat for us. He was finally successful and is now in the process of fixing up a Tahiti ketch and preparing her for another nautical adventure to wherever the sea takes us. I look at this as fate since we are both "water" signs astrologically. It is our destiny to explore the sea and her ports.

———————

Within the last year, through weekly therapy with Dr. O'Connor, I discovered I have been "fear-based" throughout my life and I need to be "faith based." During these fifty-some years of my life, armed with a religious education, I thought I had a strong faith, but being brought up by parents who were never there for me has taught me that it is only natural to feel fear and uncertainty as my basic feelings. Learning to let go of the fear and turning the consequences over to my Higher Power can provide a great feeling of relief. I just need to trust that I *can* let go of this fear. This is an outgoing and constant effort on my part. It certainly doesn't come naturally. The most magnificent lesson of my Alcoholics Anonymous Program has been to be gentle and good to myself by giving up the abuse of addiction. Slowly as I grow and evolve I've learned to love and trust myself and then learned to love and trust others. I appreciate the benefits I've brought to myself because I was willing to stop the abuse. I have a loving, generous husband who is honest and hard working. Because of his continuous hard work, we have been blessed with the opportunity, to travel all over the world and to know the security of our lovely and cozy little home.

For me, life is the journey of hope and courage and faith in God. I hope my story encourages you to meet your challenges and to find love and acceptance of yourself, no matter what circumstances you face. I encourage you to tell your story and to wait for "your" miracle to happen, because it will happen. It really will, so please don't give up.

Mabalo

www.ingramcontent.com/pod-product-compliance
Lightning Source LLC
Chambersburg PA
CBHW021635120626
46545CB00002B/550